Acclaim for Linda Spalding's

Who Named the Knife

"This arresting work follows two women, their lives shaped by very different forces, who found themselves at common intersections time and time again." —*Entertainment Weekly*

"Fascinating. . . . Part true crime, part memoir, and part contemplation of prison and the women consigned to it."
—*The Wichita Eagle*

"Intriguing." —*Los Angeles Times*

"Linda Spalding and Maryann Acker's lives are light-years apart, one a successful writer, the other a convicted killer. Yet in Spalding's penetrating, layered book . . . they are eerily connected, seen through costly, split-second turns of fate in their pasts." —*The Seattle Times*

"Haunting. . . . An intimate look at the gray areas of human nature." —*The Honolulu Advertiser*

"Compelling.... Achieves its greatest impact when the reader sees how Maryann becomes the lens through which Linda views herself."
                                                              —*Salem Press*

"Splendid.... A story that's certain to resonate strongly with readers everywhere."
                                       —*The Free Lance-Star* (Fredericksburg, VA)

"A sometimes painful and always surprising voyage of personal rediscovery."   —*The Globe and Mail* (Toronto)

"Spalding is a gifted prose stylist."   —*Ottawa Citizen*

Linda Spalding

Who Named the Knife

Linda Spalding was born in Kansas and lived in Mexico and Hawaii before immigrating to Toronto in 1982. She is the author of three critically acclaimed novels, *Daughters of Captain Cook*, *The Paper Wife*, and (with her daughter Esta) *Mere*. Her nonfiction book *The Follow* was shortlisted for the Trillium Book Award and the Pearson Writers' Trust Prize. She has been awarded the Harbourfront Festival Prize for her contribution to the Canadian literary community.

Who Named the Knife

Who Named the Knife

A TRUE STORY OF MURDER AND MEMORY

LINDA SPALDING

Anchor Books
A Division of Random House, Inc.
New York

FIRST ANCHOR BOOKS EDITION, OCTOBER 2008

The courtroom testimony quoted here was obtained by Maryann Acker's lawyer from
the Hawaii District Attorney's office.
All original material—transcripts, letters, and conversations—is as it originally
appeared, complete with spelling, grammar, and word choice errors.

The Library of Congress has cataloged the Pantheon edition as follows:
Spalding, Linda.
Who named the knife : a book of murder and memory / Linda Spalding.
p. cm.
1. Acker, Maryann. 2. Acker, Maryann—Trials, litigation, etc. 3. Spalding, Linda.
4. Murder—Hawaii—Case studies. 5. Trials (Murder)—Hawaii—Case studies.
6. Jurors—Hawaii—Biography. I. Title.
HV6533.H3S63 2007
364.152 30922969—dc22 2007001937

Anchor ISBN: 978-0-307-27920-0

Author photograph © Helen Tansey
Book design by Soonyoung Kwon

www.anchorbooks.com

Printed in the United States of America
10 9 8 7 6 5 4 3 2 1

For Michael

Justice had been done,
and I belonged to the nation of criminals. . . .

—Peter Handke, *Across* (1986)

Honolulu

1

Murder. In such a place.

From above, from the highway, it looks like a planet must have fallen into it, the round bowl edges of this bay are so perfect. Below the surface of the water, amazing fish can be seen living their lives in the coral. This is a place where children play in the waves, where parents sit on the sand, where people float, looking down. A swimmer can pause, roll over, blink a few times, and look up at the hills that surround this blue water. The hills feel protective, a barrier between the world of invention and this place.

So it must have looked to Larry Hasker in the last minutes of his life. He had been casual with his captors. "So this is a robbery? I can't believe it." He got out of the car with his shirt unbuttoned, his rubber slippers moving over the rocks. Up at the cusp, above the parking lot, the terrain is rough. Even through the slippers, he must have felt the jolts of stone and brush and dirt. He had smoked a joint in the car. He was young, twenty years old, and almost relaxed. On a ridge within sight of the highway, he turned and looked down. It was past midnight in the month of June, 1978.* The moon was high. It threw its reflected light on the ocean, so that the water looked like metal heated over flame. Molten. He breathed in and reached down for himself, opened his fly. Looking at water and night. The stars were there, too. And his captors.

There is no shame in dying with a shirt open or pants, dying in the act of emptying oneself. In such a place.

The girl who discovered the body was taking a walk before work, noticing the dusty smell of kiawe above the bay, the pungent smell of seaweed, the smell of a place where ocean and land meet. It was early in the morning, and when she saw a slipper lying in the brush, she was not surprised. Near any beach, such a forgotten slipper is not unusual, although this one wasn't broken; its thong was intact. She saw the slipper and then she saw a human foot covered in flies. It was a Monday morning and nobody was there to hear, but she screamed.

So it begins with a body on the side of the road that leads from Hanauma Bay to the Kalanianaole Highway on the windward side of O'ahu—this story of murder, on the island where I lived. The body was lying twenty-five feet from that highway among rocks, thorns, and brush. The shirt was untorn. There were no scratches, no bruises, no cuts on the flesh. There were just two wounds: one on the right side of his head and one on the outside surface of a leg.

What happens in such a place, on such a beach, is quickly forgotten in any season. What happens can so easily wash away. Even above the tide line, far above it, a third bullet can get lodged in the sand, can be plucked at by birds, can be sent down

* Please see chronology on pages 253–56.

the slope by a vagrant wind. A body can be ignored until it is past recognition, until its bones and teeth must be studied; it can be eaten; it can merge with the elements; it can be nosed at by wandering dogs. But this is a beach for children and families, a place to be walked along and sat upon. And what is there left of Larry Hasker here? Blood. Piss. A fragment of rubber slipper. He'd stood in the brush above the sea with its luminous sheen. One of his slippers had fallen off. He'd turned, unzipped, and zipped. Then he'd been shot.

Once in an ankle. Once in the head.

Someone, it must have been, with lousy aim.

2

In 1978, I was living on the windward side of O'ahu with my two daughters. I was a single mother running a child-care agency for low-income families, and I must have read about the murder of Larry Hasker in the morning paper. Another syndicate killing, I must have thought.

In those days, the morning paper was stuffed in my mailbox before I got up. I had to walk across the front yard in whatever I had worn to bed and step on the sleeping grass, which stung my feet. I'd have made myself a pot of coffee and given myself until ten o'clock to get to work because it was summer and I was my own boss. I'd have sat outside on the patio of the first house I'd ever owned—a house hard-won and loved by me as no other. I'd have sat on one of the two basket chairs and read about the murder and I'd have thought about my father, who had been dead for seven years. I'd have thought about him and about my brother, who had taken me out to Hanauma Bay in the summer of 1958.

Hawaii was still a territory then, not yet the fiftieth American state, and to my vivid fourteen-year-old imagination, it was a magical place with its ancient stone temples called *heiau* still visible in the tall grass. Skip was stationed in the Coast Guard with his wife and their new baby. He was ten years older than I was, and by the time I could measure anything, he'd left home to study. He would not be a lawyer like our father, or drink highballs, or wear a suit. He would be an architect. He would be artistic. Maybe he took me to Hanauma to teach me courage, because we both knew the brooding temper in our Kansas house.

In those days, the bay formed its own remote reality. There were other swimmers, but not many, and Skip could dive deep with nothing but his mask on, blowing the water out when he resurfaced. The waves pushed and pulled, throwing me against the coral reef, but he told me to relax and breathe, to go with the waves. And once, we were looking down through our masks when I saw something in a crevasse where the water was not even very deep. It was a moray eel curled and ready to strike, with a cold, blank look over an open throat and murderous teeth.

When I married, I moved with my husband to Hawaii, where he had been born and raised. My mother said I had fallen in love with Philip because I wanted to go back; but we had met at school and until he left me, I thought we were perfectly matched. When Philip moved out, when he started another family, I stayed in Hawaii and raised our two girls. We used to go to Hanauma Bay with our snorkels and fins. I have a picture of a birthday party there, with little girls wearing paper crowns. Now there had been a murder in that unblemished place.

3

Four years later, when I was summoned for jury duty, I had forgotten about the body lying under kiawe trees in the thorny brush above Hanauma Bay. It was 1982 and I was one of a pool of people who would be questioned by lawyers—both prosecution and defense—for any one of several trials. I was working for public television by then, across the mountains in Honolulu, and I was glad to be called. It would mean double pay, for one thing, but there were other reasons that were more personal. I was about to move to Canada with my daughters. I had met someone and I was ready to give up the house, the job, the dog, everything. But this would be a last chance to leave a little mark of myself on the island where I had lived for fourteen years. And it was a chance to test myself on my father's professional ground.

For two days, I sat with seventy potential jurors, all of us being questioned about our backgrounds and habits and beliefs in a process known as voir dire, which means "to tell the truth." Lawyers on both sides tried to weed out jurors who were likely to vote against them. Each of us was carefully studied.

"How do you feel about guns? . . . about welfare? . . . What do you do for a living?"

During those two days, I was challenged by the prosecutors of two separate trials and sent back to the jury pool. I thought I knew why. I was an outsider, a haole; I'd been an activist. I worked for public television. I was the daughter of a trial lawyer. An elderly friend said that in his opinion smart people didn't belong on juries. And a middle-aged man in the jury pool seemed to agree. He told me that what the court wanted was uneducated people, "the ones who maybe don't have the knowledge of right and wrong."

On the third day, the remnants of the pool—those who had not yet been selected—were called into a murder trial. "Will you convict based upon the testimony of a single witness?" the prosecutor asked. The question was put to each of us individually while the defendant was sitting in front of us. She was young and stunningly pretty. Her pale blond hair framed an intelligent face behind large horn-rimmed glasses. WANTED SEX AFTER KILLING one headline had read in the morning paper.

"The fact that the defendant is a woman, would you hold that against her?"

"The fact that the defendant is haole . . ." The word means "white." Like me.

At the side of the old stone Judiciary Building, there is a porch where we used to stand during breaks in the long process of questioning. Like the building itself, this porch is solid, with a feeling of dark in its corners, and I was standing out there looking at the grass that stretched away to the sidewalk when I saw a friend walk by. She was a former prosecutor and friend of my former in-laws. She was a piece of my past, part of what I was leaving. "Oh," she said when she saw me, "there you are. I heard you were in the jury pool. I hear you keep getting dismissed." She'd been up in the DA's office, visiting her former colleagues.

I shrugged. She knew I was not supposed to discuss what happened in the courtroom.

"Actually, I know the reason you haven't been chosen," she went on recklessly. "Everyone in the office noticed it. You stare. At the defendants. You make too much eye contact."

I said, "Well, I'm on my third try."

"Which case?"

She knew the rules. I mumbled, "It's a murder trial."

"*Mon dieu*. The Acker case? She's vicious, that one! She's in prison on the mainland for the same thing!" She held up two fingers. "Two murders at the tender age of eighteen. Her husband's involved, too."

"So they don't know *she* did it."

"Doesn't matter," my friend said. "They'll put her away."

Back inside, I felt queasy. Suppose they asked, during voir dire, if there was any reason I could not be a fair and impartial juror? *Doesn't matter. They'll put her away.* But when my turn came for questioning, the prosecutor had run out of allowable challenges. And that afternoon, with fourteen other people, I stood up shyly, as if I'd been invited out on the floor to dance. I was the second alternate out of three.

4

From the start, I kept a notebook, writing something like letters to Maryann Acker, as if I thought we might meet someday and talk about her trial. I addressed her directly in my notebook, but sometimes a little angrily. This was because I was sitting in a courtroom in the old stone courthouse in Honolulu, where I had lived for long enough to feel I belonged. I was born and bred in Kansas, but I had married the great-grandchild of missionaries who sailed around the Horn, disembarked in Honolulu, and stayed.

March 18, 1982

When they first read the charges—when they introduced you to us—I could not believe you were a murderer. Your muumuu is light blue and then that white bodice with its little string at the back, its little drooping tie, gives the impression of something worn in a hospital. In front of you there is a pad of paper and you write at your own pace, as if you follow your own thoughts and not the words around us. As if you might be writing to your mother, only what could you say?

Watching Maryann, I kept thinking about my divorce hearing, when Judge Chou, in his black robe, had looked down at me the way Judge Au was looking down at her. I kept remembering the way Philip's lawyer had tried to trick me into admitting that I had no right to child support—"Has he ever supported you?"—and the way I had thought that any minute all of them—the lawyers and the judge—would suddenly confess that the whole thing was a terrible joke. Did I honestly think he wanted the engagement ring back? I remembered the way I had wanted my father there. But Philip had waited to leave until the week my father died.

I had to remind myself that this was Maryann's trial, not mine.

We had settled ourselves in the jury box, but I kept my eyes on the halo of pale hair around Maryann's face. When the prosecutor stood up to introduce herself, there was a sudden, rare burst of thunder, like gunfire, as if she had planned it for effect. "Jan Futa," she said, as the shades at the top of the windows clattered and the courtroom went dark. Our prosecutor was small and delicate. She said she was going to produce an eyewitness to the crimes. "The state will prove," she said slowly, enunciating every word, "that, in addition to other crimes, Maryann Acker killed Lawrence Hasker on June 19, 1978."

Futa's long hair was pulled loosely back and tied with a dangling scarf. She wore a severely tailored suit, dark blue with a stripe, and had buttoned the jacket all the way to the top. The only decoration she allowed herself was a thin gold bracelet on the right wrist. And she always carried a gold pen in her right hand. It proved, she told us in this opening statement, a belief in something unprovable. She believed that if the pen were not there, between index and middle fingers, she would be lost.

And so, presumably, would be her case. As she explained the multiple charges—kidnapping, burglary, murder in the first degree—I was busy looking at Maryann. There were the heavy glasses, round and dark-rimmed, through which she stared at the table in front of her.

When it was her lawyer's turn to address us, the thunder had stopped. "Stephen Hioki," he said, dipping his head and holding his hands behind his back as if he expected someone to put handcuffs around his wrists. He was tall for an Asian man, with bony arms that stuck out of the sleeves of his jacket. What he would show, he said, was the state's lack of evidence. "What the defense intends to show is that Maryann was the companion of a murderer."

Her husband's involved, too.

5

The first witness, on that first day of the trial, was a man who had been kidnapped and taken to Hanauma Bay a few days before Larry Hasker was killed. His name was Joe Leach. He said he'd met Maryann at the Garden Bar in the Hilton Hawaiian Village in Waikiki on June 9 and offered to buy her a drink. A margarita, he said it was. He said they'd danced—he didn't remember how many times—and she'd told him her brother was with her and needed a ride. Could he help her out? Then maybe she and Joe could be alone for a while?

Jan Futa pointed at someone in the front of the courtroom. "Is this the man she called her brother?"

Leach said, "That's him," and we took a good look. William Acker was thirty-two years old, with a pretty face and a wiry build. Even sitting still, he seemed slightly magnetic, and he looked back at us with an off-center grin. But Leach went on testifying and we turned our attention to the witness stand.

Joe Leach told the court that Maryann had seemed calm as the three of them walked to his car, although he did not know what she was feeling inside. He said William had climbed in back but that Maryann had gotten in the front. They had used false names. He did not remember what names they had used, but William's hair had been black that night. He said William had been quiet and then he'd pulled a gun, and after that it was all obscenities, as if he wanted to make it clear how serious this was going to be. As if he were making monster faces in the dark of the backseat. Leach said he could feel the gun at his hairline. He was trying to follow the directions he was getting, but it was a Honolulu night—stars, the bright lights of Waikiki, the sound of the tide beating against the traffic—and the girl and the man didn't always agree. There was the smell of salt in the air and sweaty flesh, the three of them taking the turns, stopping at the crosswalks in front of red lights. What they told him to do was to drive to Hanauma Bay, and he took Kalakaua as far as he could through Waikiki, but the man kept yelling, "He's doing this on purpose, the fuckinshitheel! He's trying to get us lost!"

In the front, Maryann tried to calm him down. She turned to the back and said, "I think he's trying his best. Really."

Leach switched course then and drove past the golf course, past Aina Haina, and on along the moon-bright ocean, which stretched forever on the passenger side of the car. The drive took no time. Time had stopped. It stretched, then shrank, then disappeared. He couldn't describe how uneven it felt. He remembered that he hadn't been able to focus on anything but the two lanes of highway.

At Hanauma, he drove down to the parking lot, but there was a car there, so he turned back up toward the highway and, near the top, he put his foot on the brake. For a minute, they all sat there. A minute of hard breathing. His wallet had been taken during the drive. It didn't matter. Eighty dollars. His camera, too. The girl had taken her panty hose off, which was strange. Now the man ordered him out of the car. "Keep walking. Keep on." Around the bay all that crumbling and all of it steep, Maryann following them down a slope, sometimes slipping. The man told her to use her panty hose to tie Leach's hands, but she said she couldn't; she said she didn't know how, so the man handed her the gun and told her how to use it. Next he cut the sleeves off Leach's shirt with a knife. He called the knife "Justice." Leach was shaking. He watched Maryann holding the gun, and wondered what kind of people would name a knife.

6

Joe Leach had been tied up and gagged and abandoned under the kiawe trees, but he managed to free himself and hobble up to the highway after his captors drove away in his car. He got himself all the way to the Hawaii Kai police station, which was three miles distant, and someone there took off his gag and listened to what he had to say.

A few days later, Detective Jimon You at the Homicide Division in Honolulu was going through recent police reports, looking for clues to the murder of Larry Hasker. Two wounds. Two bullets. There had been a string of syndicate killings, including the murder of the district attorney's nineteen-year-old son, who had been taken to Waimanalo Beach late one night and shot in the head. Chuck Marsland was Hawaii's first elected DA and he'd run an anticrime campaign for obvious reasons. Now he was demanding action. He wanted a killer; he wanted a quick conviction.

When Jimon You found the police report filed in Hawaii Kai on June 10, he read it carefully—the details about the sleeves, especially, because Hasker's body had been found near the remnants of another man's shirt—gray, with a black design. Joe Leach was brought in. He told his story again and then again. Drawings of his kidnappers were made according to his descriptions and published in the papers. A man and a woman. Young. White. But four years went by before a sheriff called from L.A. with information. Now Maryann Acker was on trial and her husband was the prime witness for the state.

All weekend, I thought about the trial. At night, I dreamed that I was on the witness stand. I was the prosecutor; I was the defendant. I stood to argue and question; I sat to answer and defend. When I was standing, I addressed my energies to the twelve people on my right. When I was sitting, I paid close attention to the questions and tried to forget the jury. Number twelve was a blond haole, very glamorous. Number eleven was a young Japanese Hawaiian. Number nine, the only haole man, kept to himself. Like me, he'd probably lived in the islands for a long time. (As a group, we were a fair representation of Hawaii's ethnic mix.) The first juror in the top row—number eight—was about fifty, part Hawaiian, with tattoos on his arms. He had several kids, straight black hair. Next a nurse, Japanese, in her forties, who was always making a spectacle of herself, being loud. Number four was young and smartly dressed. High-waisted pants. Asian and Portuguese. There are some I've forgotten, but one of them, Mr. Sugai, had answered a question during voir dire by saying he couldn't possibly be impartial because of his beliefs about handguns. "I believe anyone who carries a gun must intend to use it." That time, the defense had run out of challenges and, like me, Mr. Sugai had to be given a seat in the jury box.

Were we a jury of Maryann's peers? I was the only one in

the courtroom who could even imagine her childhood. I was thirty-eight years old, but I had come out of midwestern middle America; our upbringings must have been similar. Now I was friendliest with the other female alternate. We paired off for lunch and often spent recesses together. We were both thinking about what we had heard, although much of it made no sense. "Rule 403," Judge Au might say. Evidence was put forward, then dropped, never mentioned again. The testimonies were confusing, and I was glad of this new friend's company, although we didn't discuss our thoughts. The previous Friday, she had run off for lunch with her husband and I had settled for tacos and a plastic bowl of refried beans on the courthouse grass. Two blocks away, at the end of the street, I could see a four-masted schooner, all rigging and lines against the sky. Looking toward the other end of the street, I could see the white columns of the palace, home of Hawaii's short-lived monarchy. I was thinking about that morning's evidence. We'd spent an hour looking at photographs and diagrams. There were color pictures of Larry Hasker's body at the murder site and at the morgue. What affected me most were the clear plastic bags, which held a red plaid flannel shirt, brown corduroy pants, underwear, and a pair of rubber slippers. After four years, those objects still seemed too intimate to be looked at by us, and I was glad they were not taken out of the bags.

From the courthouse, it was easy to walk down to the palace grounds, where the Royal Hawaiian Band plays at noon on Fridays. A nice hula, and Healani Miller singing "Kaulana o Hilo" to the strains of the band. When Hawaii's last king, Kalakaua, was crowned here in 1883, he allowed the hula to be danced for the first time since its suppression by the missionaries. Now, when the band played "Aloha 'Oe," everyone stood up, even the tourists.

Then, back in the courtroom, the girl who had gone for a walk four years before told about finding the body, except that, as she spoke, it was no longer "the body," but "him." She kept saying "him." Next, Larry Hasker's father was called to the stand with something unnameable in his face, and suddenly I wanted to jump up and grab Maryann. She stared at the father and at Larry Hasker's best friend and at the girl who had found the body. She stared at the sister, whose name was Kimberly. These were clear, detached stares with an ounce of "Fuck you" in them.

March 19

Today, when Larry's father came in, Mr. Hasker senior, when he glanced at you and then sat staring, only pulling his eyes away when the prosecutor demanded his attention, I thought I could actually see the thin, transparent membrane that separates the accused of this world from the accusers. As Mr. Hasker spoke about his son, I wanted to throw myself at you. I could see your face pushed down, my hands around your neck. I could see your tongue sticking out, your legs kicking. Sullen, brutal bitch.

It had never occurred to me before that the reason we kill murderers is that they have this effect on us—of making us murderous.

7

It was King Kamehameha who proclaimed the first law against murder in Hawaii, and he used witnesses to test innocence or guilt, exactly as we were doing. This happened almost a century before King Kalakaua wrote the national anthem and allowed his people to revert to the old ways by performing the hula. First, Kamehameha united the islands, murdering thousands of warriors in the process. In the last, great battle, he cornered them on the high Pali that separates the island's windward and leeward sides and the O'ahu defenders leaped to their deaths. King Kamehameha was a brilliant stategist. He established a system of taxation for his large kingdom that recompensed governors, district chiefs, and village headmen. He created a hierarchy, with himself as the supreme ruler. If there was a disagreement, since all of the ancient *kapus* were still in place and the number of criminal offenses was vast, Kamehameha was the final arbiter. In front of his grass house, he gathered witnesses in a circle while the accused was told to hold his hands over a calabash of water. If the hands trembled, the person was found guilty.

That was the start of the sweet but short-lived monarchy, which was conquered—years later, in 1893—when the American plantation owners brought out their guns and flags and took over.

8

On Tuesday, March 23, my daughter Esta went into town with me because Philip was going to pick her up at the courthouse. We had time to go into the lobby for a snack, and while we were standing there, Maryann was brought through— the accused, passing near enough, *in her shackles and handcuffs,* that we could have touched her.

We bought a muffin and a bread pudding from the blind woman who worked the coin machine and microwave oven and kept tabs on all the ice cream, drinks, candy, and snacks. When someone asked for a newspaper, she said that they were all gone, having counted the number sold. "Blind justice," I told Esta, then I introduced her to my alternate-juror friend, who promised to have lunch with me later, when we would sit at Heidi's, outside in the cold wind. But for most of the day, we would listen to Maryann's husband, who was the prime witness for the state. For most of the day, he would be a little cocky, but charming. "This time I must get it right. I want to tell the truth the truth the truth." High-strung and eerily sexy, William Acker kept looking at us and smiling his contagious grin. Spousal immunity is part of American law. Husbands and wives cannot testify against each other, being considered incapable of objectivity. But in Hawaii, this law had been overturned the year before.

Had they done it to catch Maryann?

When William took his place on the witness stand, the prosecutor began by establishing facts. William had been born in Illinois in 1950 and had grown up in Paramount, California. He'd met Maryann Bray in Phoenix in April 1978 at Arizona Hardware, where she was an Accounts Receivable clerk. He was just out of jail, recently paroled to his sister, and he got a job working in the hardware company's warehouse. "Correct?"

"Yes, ma'am."

"And what were you doing there?"

"Shipping clerk."

I tried to imagine being eighteen and seeing William saunter over to my desk. I'm at work, my head bent over some receipts, and I look up and there is that off-center smile, that sloping hello. I could imagine dropping my pencil and hoping my hair was okay. I remembered Philip in his checked lumber jacket the first time I saw him. We were in a college bar called The Sink. He was standing by the door, using the pay phone, and my heart almost stopped.

"When is it that you were married?"

"April 29, that same month."

"And why did you and your wife leave Arizona?"

"Lot of bill collectors knocking on the door." William grinned.

"What kind of bills?"

"She had this bank card that enabled her to write checks, buy things, you know." He shrugged. "There was nothing in the bank, but it was a guaranteed card. Even if you perhaps didn't have money in the bank, you could still use it."

William made me want to take him home and feed him a steak.

"Now how did you buy the tickets to come to Hawaii?" Jan Futa's face was alive with quizzical looks.

"With that guaranteed card."

"And what is it that you brought with you?"

"Luggage and a gun and a knife and things that belonged to us."

Keeping her head down, Maryann made notes on a piece of paper and never once looked at the man she must once have loved. The prosecutor took William through their first hours in Hawaii, when one of "the luggages" was lost. "What was in that piece of lost luggage?"

"The knife. Also a .38 revolver."

"Can you describe it?"

"It was a snub-nosed Smith & Wesson."

"And the knife?"

"Yes, ma'am. Justice."

"So you got that piece of lost luggage back." Futa was twirling the gold pen between her fingers like a tiny wand. "And after you moved to the Makiki Arms here in Honolulu, what were you doing to make a living?" The apartment Maryann shared with her husband in 1978 was just around the corner from the place my brother had lived with his wife and baby. I knew the neighborhood: Punchbowl, the ancient crater, and the Chinese cemetery I used to walk around that long-ago summer when I was fourteen, looking at the narrow stones with their calligraphy. Sometimes I was taking care of my nephew, but usually I was dreaming, pulling the spirits of that place into my bones, up through my feet. Maryann must have walked there twenty years later, when I was living in Kailua with my girls.

"She made me feel pretty bad. We didn't have nothing to eat and no job. So we discussed robberies." William was oddly childlike. "Yes, ma'am. I wanted to rob people who wanted to buy narcotics, kind of like a sting or a burn. The reason is that's what I wanted to do."

"And why is it that you chose that plan?"

"Because it's pretty safe in two ways. It was easy to live with. And, you know, plus what are they going to tell the cops: I wanted to buy some dope and he ripped me off?"

"And when you say easy to live with, what do you mean?"

"It's hard for me to pull robberies, you know. It's hard to initiate force or violence." The prosecutor was showing us William's soft side. "I didn't want to influence her; I didn't want her to influence me. It had to be right. And she convinced me that it could be right to go ahead."

Jan Futa asked what had happened when Maryann met Joe Leach in the Garden Bar, and William shrugged. "I romanced some chick walking by and went and danced while they were dancing."

The prosecutor twirled her pen. "And how was Maryann acting toward Joe in the bar?"

"Like he had a play coming."

"What do you mean?" She tilted her head.

"Romance. Without getting gross, that's the best way I can say it."

We were not allowed to write in the courtroom, so I made notes during recess, or after we had quit for the day. I sat under a tree. Or I wrote in the car. I'd feed the meter another quarter and write before I drove home. Maybe I did this because I wanted to understand Maryann. Maybe that's why I directed the notes to her. *If you discussed robberies beforehand* . . . Or maybe I liked the feel of the pen in my hand—like the prosecutor—the feel of importance, as if the case depended on me. I was the daughter of a lawyer. I'd spent summers working in his office and hundreds of hours watching Perry Mason win cases on TV. William had two criteria for his victims. They should be involved with drugs and they should be tourists. Both Hasker and Leach were residents, but when Futa asked William about this, he said Maryann had chosen the victims. He said, "We argued a little bit."

So William had been led by Maryann.

I knew the prosecutor would be easy on him because he was her witness, but by the time she got to the murder of Larry Hasker, it was obvious that William was actually enjoying his role on the stand. "Well I thought, yeah, we'll rob him. It's something he did or something he said that let me know that he was tied in with nobody, you know. I was kind of playing with him, you know. But I had told Maryann if I leave, that means no. And I left, I told him I got to go take care of something."

"Did Maryann leave with you?"

"No. She met up with me later. She couldn't be rude and just leave. Then later we ran into him again at another disco. . . ." William paused and put his head back, as if he could find the name on the ceiling. For a long minute, he stared up and we waited. "To me it seemed like he was on his way to find us and he bought us some drinks, flashed big money, you know, and I told him, I said maybe he and Maryann could get together."

"And what was your impression as to how Maryann was feeling?"

"She wanted to rob him from the beginning. Even we argued when she came back to meet me. Wow, that guy had money, you should have stung him."

With Joe Leach, they had gone directly to Hanauma Bay, but they took Larry to their own apartment first, as if they were all going to sit down together and have a friendly drink. William said he had had second thoughts at that point.

"Because when we rob him, then he can know where we live." So, while Larry sat in the living room, William and Maryann closed the door to the bedroom and had another argument. I tried to picture it—the cheap furniture, the unmade bed, the gun on a water-stained dresser. William said the knife was in Maryann's purse. "That's where it always was. That was her role."

Back in the living room, William tied Larry up with some blue nylon cord from the kitchen. "We had both taken our shirts off. You know, it was hot. And I tied him behind his back, put his shirt on him, and told him . . . oh, he didn't think, you know, when I first pulled down on him, he didn't think he was going to be robbed. He said, Oh come on, man, or something like that. This can't be real. I assured him it was and put his shirt over him and told him to play drunk, man, in case the neighbors were out and about, like I'm helping him to his car."

This time, Maryann drives. Another difference. She drives to Larry's building and then goes up in the elevator while the two men wait in the car. I pictured her at the door, clutching the key. She must have been nervous. I remembered getting drunk at a party in Kahala and walking to the house where Philip lived with someone else. My heart was banging as I opened the unlocked door and crossed the living room floor with its *lauhala* mats. Just like ours. Even drunk, I compared their quarters to my own. They had cockroaches on the kitchen counter, a diaper in the corner, a baby in another room. In darkness, I stole into the bedroom and stood at the end of their bed. The man who had been my husband for eight years was asleep with a kerchief tied over his eyes. His left leg was curled outside the sheet. Nothing had changed except that her hair was darker on the pillow than mine. I had meant to take the engagement ring off and swallow it when he opened his eyes, but I saw his journal lying on a shelf and tucked it into my purse.

. . .

Larry and his sister live on the tenth floor of a high-rise near the university. It's a crowded building overlooking a busy inter-section. Always noisy. Maryann lets herself in. What if the sis-ter is home? On the other side of the living room, there is a bureau and in it the book where Larry hides his money. He probably sleeps on the sofa, since it's his sister's place. Maryann crosses the floor and takes the book out of the top drawer and shakes it, picking up four hundred dollars in twenties. Then she grabs a tape recorder. Larry has asked her to bring him a joint. Next, back in the car, he's smoking the joint. William has untied Larry's hands, but he's holding the gun on him when Maryann says, "Let's drive him to the bay where the other guy was."

"Did you or Maryann smoke any dope?"

"No. I think he . . . I think he was already *pau*." Finished.

In the courtroom, there was a communal intake of breath. Pidgin is our trademark, our shared code.

William was one of us.

9

On the fourth day of the trial, William described the murder. "He said he wanted to use the bathroom. His words were I want to take a piss."

"And where were you at the time?"

"I walked around him, got in the driver's seat, put on the gloves."

"And where was Maryann?"

"She was standing on the passenger side of the door with the gun."

"Then what happened?"

"She shot him, shot him."

"How many times?"

"Three."

"Where was Larry when she shot him?"

"He had finished taking a piss. He zipped up. And he turned toward her a little bit. Not to jump on her, nothing like that. In fact, he said, I'm going to fall. I told him, I know it, you're going to fall. That way you won't know which way we go."

"When you heard the shots, what did you see him do?"

"Like he was hit, like he turned and fell. He fell down where he was going to walk. He fell down, he fell down there."

"What did Maryann do after she fired the gun?"

"She just stood there. It was not what she did, it was what I did. I reached over and opened the door and told her, Get in the car. Yelled at her. Got nervous, real scared. She did it. She sat in the car. I told her, What the fuck did you do that for, you know, why? The answer was strange."

Jan Futa did not ask William what the answer was. She did not ask him why it was strange. She asked, "What did you do?"

"Turned the lights off and on trying to start the car. I forgot how to start the car. My mind was blown, it was unreal. Finally got the car started and headed in the wrong direction, not the way I wanted to go."

"And what was Maryann doing?"

"Looking at the bullets, throwing them out the window."

"Can you describe how Maryann appeared to you at that time?"

"Like I do this every day, real calm. Like: You're the macho man, what's happening with you, you know, wow. Like I misled her, like I wasn't the person she thought I was, trying to make me feel bad."

After the wrong direction and panic, Maryann and William switched places so that she could drive. This happened, William said, at Sandy Beach, where he wanted to throw the gun out, but she wouldn't let him. Instead, he took it back to the apartment and decided to hide it. "I made up my mind to leave. I was scared, I was scared." He was trying to go to the laundry room to use the phone, "But she wanted to get down."

"She wanted to what?"

"She wanted to get down. Go to bed. I told her, I made a

statement to her, What? She goes, I was blown, you know, I was freaked out." Then he added, shaking his head, "I couldn't believe it," and looked over at us.

William said he went down to the laundry room to use the phone and hide the gun. "I was calling the airlines to leave, finding out information when the flights leave. But I didn't get the right information so I just stayed there and walked around. I was trying to think, trying to get a grip on my thoughts, what to do, you know. And why, I wanted whys answered. I wanted a lot of things answered. And I couldn't answer them, only Maryann could. So I was, you know, trying to get back to reality. You know. I'm sorry I had to rob. I got back on the phone. And she tapped me on the shoulder. She says, You're leaving. . . . She said things like, Don't abandon me."

I thought of the terror I had felt when Philip left. It was summer. My father had just died. I had a two-year-old and a four-year-old and no real qualifications for earning a living. It was a terrible time. I was mad with shock and jealousy. I was heartbroken, half-sick, and crazy. I was twenty-eight years old and for the very first time I was in charge of my life. *Don't abandon me.*

"It was just unreal. And it was just real bad." Listening to William now.

"And then what happened?"

"So she realized I was just freaked out. And I loved Maryann at that time, I really did. So I made arrangements."

That morning, the same morning of Larry Hasker's death, they left Hawaii and flew to Los Angeles. William told about not sitting together on the plane, about what names they had used, and how she had brought the gun when he told her not to bring it, how she had packed it in a red plastic container, how he had tried to get away from her, going to a motel and checking in while she waited for the luggage. Later, though, she knocked on his door. She was holding the gun. He said by then he was really afraid. He told her, "I'm going. That gun is all you." To us, he said, "I hid that gun a lot from her that night."

"So from there you and Maryann were together still? Where did you go?"

"Up north."

We heard a long sigh, as if the defense attorney had already exhausted himself. Then Stephen Hioki stood up slowly, as if gathering his strength. When he said he wanted to make an objection with regard to the next area of questioning, I remembered the words I had heard on the stone lanai: *She's in prison on the mainland for the same thing!* Was that the area of questioning Futa was about to raise?

Judge Au called both lawyers to the bench, where we couldn't hear what they were saying. Hioki kept gesturing, flailing his arms and hands. Judge Au was shaking his head and Futa was standing on her tiptoes, peering over the bench as if she needed to make herself seen. I thought about Larry Hasker, whose death seemed to be more important than his life. I thought of him standing on the rough hillside, the moon high above him washing everything in its unhealthy light. Below, the ocean pulling out and out. Nearby, Joe Leach's torn shirt, gray, with a black design. Larry would fall very close to it. He would swallow the water and moon and the promises of these strangers. Swallow his entire life.

10

When I was still a child and my father was still teaching at the local law school, there was a mock trial for the students, and my father asked me to play the role of a witness. I was twelve or thirteen and I was going to try my hardest. This time I was going to get it right. I was given a piece of paper with the details of a car accident: something about a goat. Now I started thinking about the goat and that long-ago mock trial while I was sitting in the Honolulu jury box, waiting for the judge and the lawyers to finish their bench conference. First, I was thinking about Larry and his death. Then I thought of William and how hard it must be to remember pertinent facts. Then I remembered the goat. It seemed to me that I had been the driver and that I had killed the goat, although I was, of course, too young to drive. There were other witnesses. Not false witnesses, but fake witnesses. Mock witnesses. They came out of imaginary houses along the imaginary road and described the imaginary scene they had not witnessed. They did not imagine they had witnessed it, but the students were told to imagine not only that they had done so but that the goat had really existed and that the farmer who owned the goat and even perhaps loved the goat was suing the driver of the car for damages.

I dressed the way my father told me to dress and worked hard to remember the condition of the road and whether the headlights were working, although it was hard because I have an active imagination and sometimes I add on to things. I said the goat was white and that one of his horns was gone, and even as I sat there in front of those Kansas students, I couldn't remember whether I'd read that in the notes or whether I'd seen it in my mind while I was reading. I wanted so badly to get it right, but every one of the witnesses told a different story.

I held on to that thought when Jan Futa resumed her questioning and William said he had wanted Maryann to go home. "She kept making me feel that nothing I do was right." I held on to that thought when he described how they hitchhiked north, then how they suddenly changed direction, getting a ride from a young man whose name was spelled out for the court. C-e-s-a-r-i-o A-r-a-u-z-a. He was driving a Chevrolet Blazer with a stick shift, which William said he did not know how to drive. He said Maryann took the wheel so Cesario could have a nap.

"Mr. Acker, can you describe Cesario Arauza?"

"Yeah, he's bigger. A lot bigger. Mexican American."

"Now, did anything happen on the way down south?"

"With Cesario? Yeah, he was murdered."

Somewhere close to L.A., near a cloverleaf, they stopped at a restaurant and gas station and William went in to order some take-out food. He was hungry and Cesario had given him money so that he could eat. Ten dollars, he thought it was. While William waited for the food, Maryann said she wanted to take Cesario's car. "She said he was making a pass at her.

Let's take this creep's car and leave him here." William said he argued against it, the way he had argued with her about kidnapping Larry Hasker. But finally he took her to the public restroom and gave her the unloaded gun. She spent a few minutes alone in there, he said, and then got back in the car and drove off with Cesario, who looked back at William through the rear window as if he couldn't believe his luck. William forgot about the food and walked to the highway, planning to hitchhike alone, but twenty minutes later, Maryann picked him up. "Twenty minutes. Or it might have been longer. It felt longer to me." He checked the gun and saw that it was loaded. Smelled it. "I didn't think it had been fired at that point." Maryann said she had left Cesario at an on-ramp, that taking the car had been easy.

They used that car in three more robberies. For a night or two, they slept in it. Then, in Long Beach, they rented a room in a motel and William said Maryann wanted to "flame" the car. William said she went out to the parking lot and he waited for her, but she didn't come back. He said, "So I got up on the roof and I saw some squad cars. More than one. And I felt that she got arrested. I went back to the room to look for the gun. I panicked. I packed everything up in a flight bag, but I couldn't find the gun. I threw all her shit on the floor, out of her purse, looking for it. And I went upstairs by the phone. And the cops came. A lot of cop cars drove up and I saw Maryann in one of them." William stayed hidden and watched as the room was searched. When everyone had gone, he left on foot, eventually taking a Greyhound bus to Yuma two days later. There, he called Maryann's father, Bert Bray, from the bus station. "He told me that, 'Man, you got my daughter in trouble. She's in jail.'"

Charged with murder.

At Bert Bray's urging, William agreed to turn himself in. "To clear things up. Because of the bullets that were used to kill Arauza. He said hollow points, and we didn't have no hollow points except for five that came with the gun that we already used practicing in Arizona."

Remember the goat, I told myself, because William wasn't sure whether he had called Los Angeles or the Yuma police. Or maybe Maryann's father had driven him to the police station. What he was sure about was the bullets. Hollow points. He said they had never used them. Except, he said, they had had hollow-point bullets in Arizona when they were practicing with the gun. Remember the goat, because Joe Leach had said William instructed Maryann about the gun at Hanauma Bay, telling her how to use it.

11

In the spring of 1979, a few months after Cesario Arauza's murder, Detective Jimon You received a phone call from the Los Angeles sheriff's office. He was told that a man in custody there had information about a murder in Hawaii. William must have been hoping that his offer of information would lighten the California sentence he had not yet received, but perhaps Detective You had no qualms about that. What he cared about was a conviction in Hawaii. He flew to L.A. to interview William as soon as he could book a flight. "They took the victim to Hanauma Bay," he wrote in his subsequent report, "and his wife took the victim into the bushy area. The guy then said that he heard three shots; his wife returned and he asked her if the guy was all right and she replied, 'No, he's dead.' The guy also added that his wife used a .38-caliber revolver with some of the bullets being hollow points."

When Jimon You read his report aloud in the courtroom,

I noticed the incongruity. Did they have hollow-point bullets in Hawaii or didn't they? William's version of things kept changing.

Having revealed Maryann's guilt to Jimon You, William signed a plea agreement with the Honolulu DA's office. "You know," he said, describing Cesario Arauza's murder during the trial, "it went over and over and over and over and over. And it was a senseless thing."

In his California trial, William had acted as his own counsel. Now, when Jan Futa asked him if he had researched California law in order to defend himself there, he said, "Where murder is concerned, that's right."

And why had he decided to take responsibility for the Arauza murder? Why had he pleaded nolo contendere?

"Because in California they have what's called felony murder rule. When there is a crime or when two people do a crime or three and as a result of that somebody's shot and killed, stabbed and killed, hung, whatever—when they're killed, each defendant is charged with murder and held responsible."

That afternoon, around three o'clock, Stephen Hioki began his cross-examination of William. Advancing and retreating between his chair and the witness stand, he seemed tense and unprepared. After noting that William was twenty-eight and Maryann eighteen when they married and that they had known each other less than two months when Larry Hasker was shot, he said, "Now, isn't it true that prior to the marriage Maryann was a fairly close follower of the Mormon Church?"

William said, "No, that's not true."

Mormon. Everyone in the courtroom must have made something of that. One of the biggest Mormon temples in the world is on O'ahu and the Mormons are a major employer out at the Polynesian Cultural Center, although in order to get a job, you have to convert, or so the story goes. I made something of it, too. My own great-grandmother was a convert, and my family is still ashamed of her. Celestial kingdoms. The Second Coming. Polygamy. Baptizing the dead and wearing funny underwear that you never take off. The Mormons are zealots, but Hioki was beating a fast retreat. Did William recall speaking to a detective in L.A.? Did he recall saying that they had found Cesario Arauza's Blazer on the side of a California highway?

"Initially, yes."

"So you lied?" Hioki was clenching and unclenching his fists.

"Definitely. I made statements, you know, there was a lot of statements made. And sometimes memory was better and sometimes it wasn't. But going back to the initial statement," William continued calmly, "I lied tremendously. That's when I was going to fight the robberies and murders." He paused. "I didn't know about the murder. I mean, I knew, but I did not. . . . I was positive it wasn't ours because of the hollow points that killed him. We didn't have any hollow-point bullets. But I was going to evade the robberies, you know. And I talked pretty good. . . ."

"And you were going to fight them by lying?"

"Well, a convict or a criminal doesn't tell the police the truth."

Someone in the courtroom laughed.

Had William ever bought bullets at GEMs in Honolulu?

"Yes."

"Isn't it true that you purchased these bullets for the purpose of sending a bullet a day to a neighbor in Arizona to intimidate him?"

"That's what I told the detective, but it's not true."

"Hadn't these people accused you of stealing their .38-caliber revolver?"

"I heard mention of that, yeah. But the fact is Maryann stole that gun. She knew where it was."

Hioki introduced two letters and asked William to examine them. "Do you recognize the handwriting, Mr. Acker?" He was making himself sound forceful, as he had probably been trained to do in law school.

"It appears to be mine unless somebody's a real good forger."

This time, everyone laughed.

Hioki read the letters aloud. To Bert Bray, Maryann's father, William had written: "What can I say? I got what I had coming. I tried a twisted plan concerning Hawaii, hoping they would offer Maryann deals. But instead, I will catch the Hawaii charges. In fact, I've already told the Attorney General I would cop to the Hawaiian affairs. . . ." Hioki asked him to explain.

"I believe," William said, scratching his neck, "this was when I was going to cop to everything. I might have told this to Bert Bray. But I also bullshitted Bert Bray a whole lot because he did me too."

The second letter was to Maryann, although William had addressed it to "Free," which he said was his name for her "because of her ability to stay out of jail at that time." He had written: "Honey, I couldn't tell you then, nor can I fully explain now. But the two heavy things that went down were mine to take. I will explain when I can, sister of mine in the Randanian way." Hioki paused. He said, "What did you mean by that?"

William said, "It's a step beyond Ayn Rand. It's taking her a step further than she goes. It's a philosophy."

"Doesn't this philosophy basically mean you look out for yourself first and foremost?"

"No. It basically means you are yourself."

Hioki closed his eyes. Then he opened them and returned to the letter. But I was watching his narrow face, his chin like a spoon, his eyes humorless. He was shaking the letter as if it contained loose dirt. "You indicated that as far as you know, it was Maryann who killed Mr. Arauza, is that right?"

"Yes."

"Isn't it true that the day after Mr. Arauza was killed you told a Mr. Raymond Guillen that the orange and red spot on your pants was from the blood of a man you had just killed the day before?"

"No. That's not true."

Hioki dropped the question and we were never to hear another word about the pants or the blood or the identity of Raymond Guillen. When Hioki jumped back to Phoenix and asked why William and Maryann had left—was it to evade William's parole officer?—the question was stricken. Once, William corrected Hioki bluntly. "No, no. Read my lips." When Hioki mistakenly referred to William as Mr. Leach, William said flatly, "I'm not Mr. Leach." Hioki said, "Sorry. I'm sorry." But William was becoming belligerent. When asked about the Hasker murder, he told Hioki they'd never gone to Larry's apartment. Then he said they went to Larry's apartment first, after the bar, and then to their own. Then he said, "You're not listening to me. We went to our apartment, the gun was pulled on him, then we went to his apartment because he said he had cocaine and money."

"Okay," said Hioki. "Okay."

"You understand that?"

"Okay."

"I told you. Now, listen to me real carefully, watch my mouth."

Stephen Hioki did not look at William; he looked down at his notes. He said, "You indicated during direct examination that you represented yourself in the California case, is that correct?"

"Yes I did."

"And you researched the area of law concerning murder, is that right?"

"And robberies."

"And based on your research you decided that you should

plead guilty because under California law you were responsible
for that particular incident, isn't that right?"

"Just as responsible."

Suddenly, Maryann's lawyer slipped out an invisible knife.
"And can you explain, Mr. Acker, why you were sentenced to
life without parole?"

Futa leaped to her feet. "Objection!"

The judge sounded alarmed. "I'll see counsel in chambers,"
he shouted, banging his gavel. Then he called a recess, telling us
to disregard Hioki's remark. But how could we? And what did
Hioki want us to know about William? That he had nothing to
lose, so he would swear to anything? But why not this: that he
had nothing to gain . . . that he was therefore telling the truth?

Life without parole.

I tried to imagine it.

The point was not to take everything personally, although I
got stuck on the thought of my great-grandfather, who ran off
to Yuma and tried to start a new life. He'd left his wife and children. Everything. Burned the last bridge. Now I began to think
of William as my unfortunate relative. My history.

I went straight home that night, and Michael was there, waiting. We had started our new life together with his five-month
teaching visit to Hawaii. That night, and every night, I went
home to Michael and Esta and Kristin and whatever had happened in their day. I went home to the dog and cat, to the
house, to the garden that needed attention, to a dinner that had
to be made. I went home to the newspaper, which was full of
holes since Michael cut out any articles about the trial. I was
careful not to listen to the radio or watch the news on TV. But
there were voices in my head still talking to me. I'd be standing
over Esta, watching her do her homework, and I'd remember
some line of questioning: "And after the robbery of Mr. Leach,
did she want sex then?"

I'd be standing in the kitchen, putting the dishes away, and I'd hear William's answer: "Are you trying to exploit Maryann's sex life or mine?" which was nothing compared with his confusing responses about the gun. Who had it? Who hid it? When? He took a walk first or maybe he didn't. He made a phone call while he was hiding it. Or he made it later. He was scared. "I didn't want nothing to do with the bitch." But he bought two tickets. They left together. They had the .38 called Little John and a knife named Justice, and five days later in California, Cesario Arauza was killed. I couldn't talk about these things that went round and round in my head. I was waiting for Maryann to be called to the stand, but what could she possibly say after everything we had heard?

12

You are as pale as the moon. Today you will take the stand. You will be a surprise package presented to us by your lawyer. But first we must finish with your husband. "The night you robbed Mr. Leach, did Maryann wear her glasses?" "No. She usually wore contacts then. Oh, Maryann could doll herself up. She didn't need a disguise. She would just change her looks."

Apparently you have only two outfits, the soft muumuu and this white dress with a tight, white jacket. The dress has an odd strap in back, visible through the light material of the jacket. Who chooses your clothes? Who cuts your hair and buys your makeup? The shoes are so high that you tip forward on the platform heels. Each time you come in from recess, you cross the room slowly, as if you are walking through water, focusing on the destination of your chair.

Kristin was in the courtroom that morning. Among the rows of observers, I could pick out her small, familiar face. At lunchtime, my alternate-juror friend and her daughter went with us to a restaurant. Kristin said, "Of course she did it, didn't she?" and "He's awful!" meaning Hioki. "Brown jacket! Green pants!"

That afternoon, Hioki called Maryann to the stand at last. He looked like he wanted to carry her up in his arms, but that wasn't necessary; she swam through the distance between her table and the judge's high bench. And then I heard her voice, which was soft and low-pitched.

"Was the knife in your purse?" Hioki asked gently.

"I don't recall."

"What name were you using that night?"

"I'm not sure."

On the stand, she seemed not so much frail as nonexistent.

I looked around now, trying to find members of Maryann's family. If I were on trial, my mother would be here, I thought. She'd bring me things to read in prison. She'd bring me books and soap. And if my father were alive, surely he'd be here defending me.

"Why was it that you came here?"

"I wanted to come and I came with him."

"Who named the knife Justice? Did you?"

"No, I did not. Bill did."

When Maryann went over the details of the Leach robbery, her voice was a whisper. Her face was bloodless. It was William who stole the gun. It was William who decided to rob Mr. Leach. When they drove to Hanauma, it was William who pointed the way. "And then Bill had him stop and Mr. Leach got out. They walked off the side of the road down the ravine. Then Bill called me and asked me to hold the gun while he tied Mr. Leach up."

"Did he instruct you on how to use the gun?"

"I don't believe so." Maryann was not going to help herself.

Hioki asked her about the Hasker murder. He said, "Where were you, Maryann?"

"In the car."

"Which seat?"

"The driver's seat."

"Then what happened?"

"Then I heard gunshots."

"Do you recall how many?"

"Two." She said William came back to the car, told her to move over, and then drove off in the wrong direction. When she asked him what had happened, he said it was just something he had to do. He stopped at a restaurant. Maryann did not want to eat. He took her home and went off to park the car. When he came back, he said he wanted to leave and went down to the laundry room.

Then the Arauza story. When it came to this second murder, she said only that William was in the backseat. He told Cesario to stop the car and get out. Again, he was holding the gun. Again, they went down a slope. She heard a shot. Again, William said it was something he had to do. She made it sound almost boring.

When Hioki asked her about being a Mormon, she said, "I was a Sunday-school teacher."

"Did you terminate that work prior to coming to Hawaii?"

"It was causing a lot of problems between Bill and I. He strongly objected. And because of him there were questions raised in my mind about the validity of my religion."

"Now, did you hear Mr. Acker use the word Randanian?"

"Yes."

"To your knowledge, who created this philosophy?"

"Bill did. He was going by the philosophy of the author Ayn Rand." Maryann was wearing the white dress, and her pale hair fell around her face. Every minute or so, she reached up to adjust her glasses, as if they did not fit her well. "It's ego-centered. Look out for yourself only. It's atheist and very self-centered." There was a darker line where her hair was parted; I could see it from the jury box. So the blond wasn't natural. I wondered how she managed that in prison. She wore only a little blush and pink lipstick. When she spoke, I watched her stillness. The relationship—it was strained. Decisions—he made them all.

"Now during the time that you were in Hawaii, did you experience any type of fear of bodily harm?" Hioki edged his way toward the witness stand, as if to remind her that the male body can be threatening.

"Yes, I did." There had been an argument in the apartment. There were a lot of arguments, but after one of them, William pointed the gun at her and the gun went off. "The bullet went right by my face."

I was listening for emotion. But there wasn't any.

13

You are always so still. You haven't twitched or smiled or frowned.

Day six and I was no longer an alternate. Juror number three was ill and I was her replacement. My friend the first alternate had already moved up. For five days, I had felt marginal, but this was better. We were voting members of the jury now. And, in order to convict, a jury must be unanimous. I would listen harder. We'd had a three-day break and Jan Futa was looking refreshed.

She started her cross-examination of Maryann by asking about Yuma, Arizona, where Maryann had finished high school. Then she asked about Phoenix, where Maryann had gone by herself at the age of seventeen. Why had she left home? Was there trouble with her parents? Wasn't she running with a fast crowd? Wasn't she frustrated by the smallness of Yuma? Only a few months after leaving home, hadn't she met William and married him? "Would you really have considered yourself a good Mormon, Ms. Acker, before you met William?" The prosecutor's questions were nicely connected, like a narrative.

"Yes," answered Maryann. Cigarettes, coffee, alcohol—everything had started with William. I tried to remember if anyone had ever affected me in quite that way. I've gone down a few dark paths, but my parents were temperate. I learned to drink and smoke at home. Our Episcopalian household had no room for purity.

Then Futa asked about the quick departure for Hawaii and the decision to stay. "You cashed in the return tickets that you and Bill had shortly after you got here, isn't that true?"

"Yes."

"And you used that cash to live on?" The prosecutor wanted us to know about Maryann's finances, to remember that she had charged two round-trip airline tickets, that she was a girl who made decisions. "And you had your bank card at that time, right? But you didn't leave Bill?" She wanted us to know that Maryann had had whatever it took to escape, that Maryann had used her maiden name to rent the apartment and later she'd used it to pawn stolen things. She'd used her charms to entrap two men. She'd held the gun on Joe Leach and driven Larry Hasker's car. Futa was steering us toward what my father would have called "a foregone conclusion," that Maryann was a willing participant in the kidnappings, the robberies.

The questions came faster and faster. "Did you hear any talking before you heard the shots?" "How long after you lost sight of them did you hear the shots?" "How quickly did one shot follow the other?" "Was it like bangbang or was it bang   bang, or how was it?"

Maryann said, "Like bang . . . bang."

When Futa brandished some papers, Judge Au peered over his glasses. "What does it purport to be? A letter?"

The prosecutor moved over to the witness stand. She smiled up at the judge and asked Maryann to identify the handwriting on the pages. Then she began to read with the hint of a smirk in her voice: " 'Honey, please don't blame yourself for what happened to us,' " she read. There was a long look at Maryann, a raising of eyebrows. " 'You tried to keep me from it,' " she went on, " 'and I was fully aware of what could happen, but I didn't want to leave.' " There was the foregone conclusion again. "Did you write that?"

"Yes."

"Did you also go on to write, 'I also realized, though, that this wouldn't have happened if I wasn't with you. I suppose I should have thought more of that also. I'm sorry sweetheart. I love you. I know that we will once again be together. Honey, this is what I want.' "

The letter had been written while Maryann was in prison in California, waiting for her trial there. It crossed my mind that she might have wanted her husband's help, might have pretended loyalty out of fear, but Futa spun around to look at us indignantly. "When you were with Mr. Leach, you were frightened, is that correct?"

"Yes."

"And do you think that when you were going through your role of enticing him, so to speak, do you think that he knew you were frightened? And with Mr. Hasker? Would it be fair to say that with both men you played your roles with them very well?"

Hioki objected that this was argumentative.

"Do you feel you were doing a good job of leading them on?" Futa continued. And of course by the end of it, when she asked, "Ms. Acker, have you played other roles in your life?" we had heard the point underlined. Maryann could look at us with her blue, blue eyes and say anything and almost be believed.

14

Eighteen years later I would find the yellow notebook. Yellow with a red spine, as if designed to be noticed. I would find it under a pile of papers in a cupboard in Toronto, almost forgotten, like the trial. In the back of the notebook were the clippings that Michael had cut out of the newspapers on the last day.

> Acker, 22, showed little emotion as the verdicts were announced, but her cheeks appeared flushed and her head dropped slightly when the murder conviction was read.

> The circuit court jurors who convicted Maryann Acker of murder yesterday

felt that it really didn't matter if she fired the fatal shot. . . .

During the seven-day trial here, the prosecution's key witness was William Acker, who also was charged with the same Hawaii crimes, except for the murder. As part of a plea agreement, he pleaded guilty to robbing Hasker and agreed to testify against his ex-wife. In exchange, the prosecution will dismiss the other counts.

There was the headline that read WANTED SEX AFTER KILLING and this: "The jurors deliberated just an hour and 45 minutes."

What we on the jury didn't know was that it was Maryann who was convicted of felony murder in California not William. She was serving a sentence of seven years to life there for being present when Cesario Arauza was killed.

For eighteen years, I had tried not to think about my part in Maryann's life. For ten of those years, I had suffered a depression so dark that at times it swallowed me. Wasn't I living with a person who loved me? And didn't I love in return? There was enough passion between us to move an entire household across an ocean and a continent. But once I got to Toronto, I seemed to have left myself behind. In the house with the tropical garden. In the interesting job with public television. In the boardrooms of my daughters' school and the Women's Political Caucus and the Literary Arts Council and a thousand other places. I had left myself in Kailua and in Manoa Valley, where I had lived with Philip. I had left myself in Puck's Alley, where I had gone for beer on hot afternoons, and at the Willow's Restaurant, where my children had fed the fish. I had left myself with all my friends, bridges gone up in smoke. If I had also left my failures—bitter endings of various kinds—the good things I had accomplished were meaningless in this new place. Who was I? What had become of my life?

In Toronto, I'd become fixated on certain things: death, murder, my incapacity to befriend. The way I run away from things. Now I turned the pages of the yellow notebook and looked at the dates. What surprised me was that I had kept writing even after the end.

April 5

It's over. Everyone at work knows I was on the jury and, of course, when I saw coworkers during the trial I laughed it off. I didn't mind describing your features and mannerisms, but I honestly didn't want to feel influenced. I wanted to decide for myself. I wanted to know I could decide. During voir dire I had said yes when asked whether I was willing to pass judgment on another human being. If I cannot judge her, I'd thought, who can?

I had imagined myself sitting in the jury room, which would look like the jury room in *Twelve Angry Men*. Everyone would be voting to convict and I would express my reasonable doubt. William was serving life without parole. He had been cocky, pleased with himself. His testimony had been elaborate, full of details, like my story of the one-horned goat. Was it believable? As a full-fledged member of the jury now, I had to be sure. I had to weigh Maryann's innocent face, her soft hair, her voice. I had to weigh her Mormon childhood, her devout parents, the strict upbringing she must have endured. I knew about teenage rebellion. I knew about trying to please a man.

Was Maryann Acker a killer?

It was time to decide.

It had become our routine, since Michael had come to live with us, to drive together through the long grasses of Kawanui Marsh on the windward side, out to the highway, and across the astonishing Pali, that sheer mountain wall where King Kame-hameha cornered the O'ahu warriors and forced them over the edge. An image of those helmeted warriors floating down-ward through the mist haunts everyone who crosses, it is so established in the histories, so sung about, so simultaneously mourned and praised, this final conquest that united all of the Hawaiian Islands. It is Kamehameha's gold statue that stands in front of the courthouse, covered in leis.

It was our practice to cross this high place, usually at a bumper-to-bumper crawl, listening to music, talking: the poli-tics of the English department, the trial, and plans for our life together in Canada. But on that last day of the trial, something was wrong with my unbeautiful, ungroomed cockapoo.

We were a few minutes ahead of schedule. We had time to drop him at the vet's before we started across the mountains for town.

But the dog had no appointment and we were told to take him back home.

It was here that a five-minute break in my life changed everything in Maryann's.

Toronto

15

The morning I found the yellow notebook, I called the court records department in Hawaii, forgetting about the time difference. Hours. Years. I couldn't wait. I had to find Maryann. On May 25, 1982, a few days before I left Hawaii for Canada, Judge Au had sentenced her to a minimum of ten years.

She would be out by now. She must be out.

While I did the laundry, I kept eyeing the clock. I walked to the store for groceries and took in the summer look of the street. All the small front gardens were blooming. I stopped to look at a neighbor's roses while I wondered what to say to Maryann. How to tell her that I was the reason she'd been convicted. I could say I broke speed limits, shoved the dog through the door, locked it again, ran back to the car. Explain that Michael had planned on coming in to watch the trial—the final proceedings—so we parked the car, and then both of us ran up the courthouse steps and into the polished hall. (I should have asked him to drop me first. Why hadn't I?) I remember the feel of the courtroom door, its smooth surface, and the eyes in the opening crack. I remember the whispering mouth of the bailiff. "You are excused. You are five minutes late." Five minutes. My pulse was furious.

Michael and I sat down with the other spectators. What I felt was rage and shame. Judge Au made his entrance. Then Jan Futa was pulling herself to her feet. Her hair was tied with a white silk scarf, as if she might be ready to wave it in surrender, but the gold pen was between her fingers, firmly in place. Robbery one! Burglary in the first degree! Kidnapping! Here she stopped and stared at the jury. "Let me remind you that it is not necessary that each element be committed by the defendant alone," she said quietly. "And there is another charge involved." Turning to point at Maryann, she let the word out slowly, as if we had never heard it spoken aloud: *Mur-der*. Both syllables clear. "Murder in the first degree." I reached in my bag and pulled out the yellow notebook with the bright red spine. I could write openly now, but the words on the page were staggering and limp. Futa argued that Maryann had had everything to gain by lying. "She had nothing to lose and everything to gain and for that reason I will submit to you that she did lie to you. William didn't have to say anything about the events in Hawaii. A year after those events, Detective Jimon You had no suspects. There is no reason for William to have fabricated these events."

Not with a sentence of life without parole.

William, she said, was virtually controlled by Maryann. "The testimony of William and Mr. Leach," Futa said, "is very close. I submit the reason for this is that it is true. Who doesn't remember what happened? Maryann Acker. Quite conveniently there are many things she doesn't remember because it's hard to fabricate things if there is no basis of truth. Mr. Leach testified that William Acker 'looked as scared as I felt.' Mr. Acker is high-strung, nervous, not calm and collected like his wife. What was she doing most of the time? Looking straight ahead. Why? Because she did not want Mr. Leach to see her."

I studied the jurors, especially the third alternate, who had taken my seat. I thought of the *heiau* on the Big Island I had visited with my parents on their last trip. It's called "the City of Refuge" because in old Hawaii a person could run there when they were about to be taken for sacrifice.

I was glad my father could not see me now.

When Stephen Hioki rose for his own summation, he told the jury that the defendant was presumed to be innocent even after everything they had heard. "Let me take you back to the time Mr. Acker was testifying," he said quickly, as if he might be about to recite the entire case. "I was asking him details—where Larry was standing, etc. If you recall, Mr. Acker got defensive, abrasive—began to assert himself through the microphone—became a wiseacre on the stand with little respect for it." He looked around the courtroom. "I had touched upon a nerve," he concluded indignantly, raising his voice by a note.

The case against Maryann Acker came down to two versions of a murder, and Hioki had tried to unravel only one of them. He had made William his adversary and never let us close to Maryann's story. In the time it took the rest of us to eat lunch, the jury found her guilty of kidnapping, robbery, unauthorized control of a vehicle, burglary, and murder in the first degree.

16

When it was finally morning in Honolulu, I spoke to three women at the Hawaii Department of Public Safety. One was in charge of interstate inmates, one was in charge of dual-jurisdiction inmates, and one referred me to the other two. None of them knew about Maryann.

Next, the Internet, where looking for her went like this:

Maryann Acker = must have
Murder = must have
Hawaii = must have
California = must have

I added "must have" in each instance because there may be other Maryann Ackers in the world, but it is unlikely she or they will have committed murder and, if so, unlikely that she or they will have committed it in both Hawaii and California.

As I was typing, the computer underlined two words as wrong: *Acker* and *murder*.

"Such a long time ago," said a woman at the California Department of Corrections, which I called next. "But wait," she said, looking through her own computer files. Then she told me that Maryann was still in prison. She was an inmate at the California Institution for Women, known as CIW, in Chino, about an hour out of L.A. Eighteen years after the trial in Honolulu, and twenty-two years after the crimes, she was still locked up not far from the place she'd been arrested in 1978.

June 28, 2000

Dear Maryann,

I was on your jury in Hawaii, but I was dismissed. I've been reading a notebook I kept during your trial and I'm wondering how you are doing.

Very sincerely,
Linda Spalding

I wrote the letter at our cottage in the country, where I was alone for three days. I had no car, no way to get out except by walking a mile to the highway and then maybe hitching a ride. There was nobody within shouting or even screaming distance. And I'd been waking up in the middle of the night with the familiar clutch—a feeling that everything was slipping away. My life. Why imagine that a woman in prison for twenty-two years would read my letter with any interest in writing back? "Won't she hate you?" a friend had asked. How, if she did answer, would I explain? "If I had been there that morning, been there on time, you'd be free." Up there in the country, the river sounds like an engine left running, like a buzz of static that is constant, rattling, each crash crashing into the next crash before the last one has finished. There are no commas, no apostrophes. Out beyond trees, spirits wander. The river was thrumming, and I called my mother, who would soon be among the spirits. I called her in order to hear a human voice. She had been out to dinner with her friend. "She does so much for me," my mother confessed. "It makes me feel dependent."

I said it was good for both of them; it works both ways.

"How's that? What can I ever do for her?"

"You provide the comfort of need."

"She has family."

"It's not the same." I said this, although lately I'd hung on my mother's words as to a lifeline. I should have recorded her, but I knew I would never replay our conversations after she died. I actually have a record of my brother's voice, but it would kill me to hear it. The dead are with me all the time. Day in, day out. Only I miss the flesh.

I grieved for my mother even as I talked to her, and little by little I gave her more of myself. "I think I have arthritis in my knee," I said that night, trusting her with this small fear for the first time.

"It's not so bad," she said. "I had it in my hands and it went away. It comes. It goes. Don't worry too much about it." Sensible and consoling words, which meant I still had a mother, thank God.

"I remember when you stopped knitting."

"Yes."

"And did it really hurt?"

"Yes. But I did something. Heat, probably, because I like heat. And anyway, it stopped. It doesn't bother me now."

"But it makes me feel old."

"Well, you aren't."

What does *old* mean, I wondered, to a woman who buried her husband when he was fifty-nine, her son at fifty-seven, and she's almost ninety? One day a few years earlier, but after my brother had died crashing his plane, she'd gone to the doctor for a checkup. I was visiting at the time, sitting at the table when she came home and burst into tears. (I'd seen her cry only three times.) "I'm absolutely fine. There's nothing wrong with me!" Her collapsed face, her collapsed expression. Shame. Horror. To have survived.

17

July 16, 2000

Dear Linda,

I received your card today, and to say I was totally overwhelmed is the understatement of the year! You, of course, have no idea what's been going on recently to cause my astonishment. I just found out last night that a Writ of Habeas Corpus *on the Hawaii case was filed last week. Then, I got your card. Today! The timing is really incredible in my opinion. I have a feeling you might have made a difference! Were you an alternate juror? Is that why you were dismissed? There are so many things I would like to ask you, but I do want to thank you, from my heart, for writing to me.*

A few months after my original sentence in Hawaii, the Paroling Authority reset my minimum term. They increased it to 30 years. That's why this writ is so important to me. I have been incarcerated for 22 years now. I was so ~~insane~~ naïve then, but feeling like

I knew all there was to know and that I could handle the world. When we arrived in Hawaii he really turned my world upside down. In my trial, I testified very truthfully. I was terrified of William and in fear for my life. Today, I see so many things I could have done. But I guess that's the big difference between being 18 and 40. I have grown so much, and learned so much about myself. Again, I sincerely thank you! I hope I will hear from you again, and please, feel free to ask me any questions you may have.

Sincerely,
Maryann

It was August by the time I got this letter in Toronto, and I carried it up to the cottage along with shorts and jeans and the yellow notebook. Driving east, I looked out at the summer countryside along Highway 401, where the corn was ripening under a silky sky. I'd moved to Canada when I was thirty-eight, coming to a place where I had no friends, no network of support, and where things with my newly constituted family were electric and complex. Overnight, my children had shed their Hawaii childhoods like embarrassing skins, and within six months I hardly knew them or myself. I had been burning bridges forever, but as I looked out at Lake Ontario, stretched like a wall between my two countries, I saw Maryann as a link to my former life.

Thirty years.

The average sentence for a felony in Hawaii is four or five. Even syndicate killers don't get more than twenty.

That night, I dreamed about her prison bed. It was iron, painted dark green. On it a colored quilt, very bright, made by someone in her family, blues and red against stark white cotton. In the dream, I admired her for possessing such a quilt, and yet I was surprised, as if I assumed we could not have the same taste. Someone in her family had made it and she kept it in her otherwise-undecorated cell. The quilt was a proclamation. The dream was about Maryann as part of a family, as part of my American past. When I woke up, I lay in bed drinking a cup of coffee and staring out at the rain, trying to remember if there had ever been a day when I woke with sufficient joy. All that came to mind were the few days of my childhood when my brother was home from college, mornings with an ecstatic murmur that wouldn't be stilled, like romantic love without a premonition of sadness. Otherwise, I looked back on mornings when I loved getting up to my girls. They were tousled, beautiful, getting ready for a dance class or birthday party.

Then I thought of my grandmother's Kansas City house, which I'd visited for a two-week period every summer of my childhood. I thought of the lovely solitude of those lost summer days, although they consist, now, in a series of images much like a dream that, when told, dissolves immediately. I suppose there was the liberation from my parents to take into account, although in all other ways the brief interlude with my grandmother was more constrained than the rest of my life. I should explain that my grandmother was deaf, that we learned, over the years, to move through our days and evenings in silent harmony, that she worked happily in her sewing room while I was left to my fantasies.

One summer, it was hotter than the ordinary hundred-plus degrees and we created a space in her unfinished basement, where we spent all our waking hours. Without her sewing machine, my grandmother embroidered or crocheted. I was embroidering something myself—a flannelette baby smock— but I painted pictures, too, and wrote stories. I filled the pages of my diary. It was harder to live in my imagination down there, with my watchful grandmother so close, but she was a woman who had lived alone for so many years that she considered it no affront to sit in silent companionship. The smock was for my brother's first child, who was yet to be born and whose short life was to be my first tragedy. But that summer, as long as I didn't move from my wicker chair, I was safe.

Now, under a window of the cottage, I had been making a garden—a vanity among all the pine trees and birches, all the grass and stone and water. Children grown and the decisive acts of my life behind me, I had been trying to believe I was in the summer of my life. The garden, small as it was, had been a laying of claim and a slight breaking of the stern rule we adopted on taking over the land: only to perch, not to civilize. When we first came up here, it was just a year after Maryann's trial, and this house, with its broken deck and pointy roof and stilts, was as precarious as we felt.

18

Her letters were handwritten. "You say that you are oddly connected to my story. Do you remember the circumstances of why you were replaced on the jury?" When I received mail from Maryann, I read the lines and then I read between the lines, because the words were so perfectly formed and spelled and punctuated. "I was so young when I got arrested. I had only been out on my own for a few months before my fateful meeting with William. There is so much I've never experienced. In some ways I feel that, emotionally, I'm still stuck at 18."

Yes. Her letters reminded me of the girl I was when I met Philip.

"I would have done the same thing if it came to a sick animal," Maryann wrote when I finally told her why I'd been thrown off her jury. "But darn that vet for at least not keeping him til the end of the day! All of that, however, is water under the bridge. One thing I have learned over the years is to learn from the past but not to dwell on all the 'what ifs.' That doesn't really serve any constructive purpose."

Constructive purpose? I sent a postcard that said: "I can't remember what was wrong with the dog. It must have been more or less serious . . . but really! It wasn't worth thirty years of your life." I didn't tell Maryann that I always dwell on what-ifs, on what the poet Tomas Tranströmer calls a book that can only be read in the dark. What if I had been on time that last morning of the trial? What if she had grown up in a different house with different parents? When I asked her to describe the house where she grew up, she wrote about her prison job. She told me about the degree she had earned. She said that, since the trial, she had been out of her prison only once, when she was driven into L.A. for a dental appointment. By then, she was nervous about going out. She was nervous about being shackled. She was nervous about seeing a strange dentist. In the van, she peered through small barred windows to look at cars, shops, and houses. What she saw was the freeway, a long slice of the present tense.

19

Late that summer, I drove back to Toronto in order to do something I had delayed, along with my guilt about Maryann, for eighteen years. I'd been living in a country I had no claim to, dividing my time between a house in downtown Toronto and one that stretches between a dirt road and a river. But finally, I had applied for Canadian citizenship. All my life, I had excused myself from membership. I had lived without affiliation or ceremony. Even my wedding to Philip was an elopement. But now I wanted something more, unlike Maryann, who would emerge from prison without attachment to anything.

Sitting across from me in the waiting room at the Department of Immigration was a young woman nursing a baby, breasts full of promise. I watched her. I was the only American in the room. After a time, when we had to line up and show ourselves with a picture ID, a Muslim woman was taken to a corner, where her *nijab* was lifted while official eyes flicked over her and checked her photograph. Two men who had come with her glared and clenched their fists. Finally, we were ushered into the room where we were to make an oath of allegiance to the queen. The doors were locked behind us. A skinny clerk in a black robe went through an hour of instructions—when to stand up, sit down. This was followed by thirty brief minutes of ceremony, during which a tape deck punched out "O Canada!"—though not without static. There were small conversations among those of us who were alternately sitting and standing: Where were you born? How long here? Could you take my picture, please, when I go up? If it is possible to be moved by the sight of a tape deck on a table, I was, though a glance at the photo of a young Queen Elizabeth made me, momentarily, wish to bolt. What would my father think of my desire to be taken in by Loyalists?

I had called my mother, having told her nothing through-out the process of application but suddenly wanting her to understand what I was doing, as if, like a secret marriage, it would otherwise be null and void. She said it was wonderful to become a citizen of Canada, where I lived, and that I had lost nothing and gained something I valued. It was not the response I had expected, but in losing her short-term memory, most of her long-term friends, and her husband and son, she had also lost the judgmental reactions that had once so intimidated me. In her old age, my mother had become the mother of my dreams.

Back at the cottage, my big orange lilies were nodding by the east wall of the house. The yellow daisies were bowing. The delphiniums were blue to a fault and petunias pushed against the rocks. It was this, exactly, that I wanted to be: fully in bloom, evident and engaged. I wanted to belong here, by the river, where I had sprinkled the ashes of my brother and his wife, where we had buried our cat and dog, where we measure our lives. The stretch of house is at right angles to the water, so that only the end where we sleep has any view of it. And the river itself makes a right-angle turn in front of us, rushing down a set of rapids, pouring over rocks and pieces of the Canadian Shield that make portaging so difficult and walking such joy.

20

When I asked Maryann about her childhood, I got three verbal snapshots; learning to whistle when she was six months old; when she was two, getting a rocking chair. "I was born accident-prone. There's a picture of me sitting in that rocking chair with a black eye." At three, it was a tricycle, which she rode into her sister's room one Christmas morning before anyone else was up. Penne was nine years older. There was a cockapoo. It was a happy family.

But there was also this: Until she was four, only two men were allowed to carry her—her father and an uncle. When any other man tried, she'd scream.

Her mother was a housewife, although she once worked as a cashier in the *Phoenix Gazette* building. "I was still young, so I'm not sure why she went to work. Whether she just wanted to or if it was financially necessary." Whatever the reason, Gladys Bray didn't work for long. She went back to baking, washing, tending her family, and serving the church community like an acolyte.

Bert was the easygoing parent. Quick to laugh, he seemed to like everyone and kept his job as a salesman for McKesson & Robbins for thirty years. Born a Baptist in Texas, he converted to Mormonism when his first child died, although it took the second son's death to get him baptized.

About those two deaths, Maryann gave me the facts as if she had given them a hundred times. The baby had swallowed a paper clip. The other son had died of an asthma attack at the age of fourteen, about the time Maryann was born. I remembered the Mormon belief about little souls waiting in heaven, that it is every Mormon mother's duty to have as many babies as possible so those souls can be reborn. I could imagine Gladys with baby Maryann, jealously guarding her every step. I could imagine her shaking her head, saying no and no and no, making too many rules. "Obedience is the first law of heaven," preaches this church. Obedience to the law of the living prophet rather than to the law of the state. I know about this because of that great-grandmother who joined the Latter-Day Saints when one of her children died. The story is that they promised to reunite her with the child, whose name was Robert E. Lee Dickinson, at the Millennium. In a fervor of hope, she moved the family out of Brown County, Kansas, where they owned thousands of acres of the richest wheat land in the world, to Independence, Missouri, where the early Saints had built their version of Zion on what Smith claimed was the original site of the Garden of Eden.

Mormons are taught that life is a test, that they have been plucked out of heaven and brought to Earth to try on the temptation of free will. Like all Mormon children, Maryann spent a large part of each week being indoctrinated. In Sunday school and once-a-week Primary, she was taught that a man named Joseph Smith had discovered twelve gold tablets in a cave in New York State in 1827. In 1823, he'd been told about the tablets by an angel named Moroni and he had later deciphered them by reading through Urim and Thummim, peep stones attached to a breastplate. "What is a peep stone?" she must have asked. And perhaps her teachers told her that it was a special kind of lens given to a select few by God. Then they would have told her that the book Brother Joseph translated—The Book of Mormon—is as divine as the New Testament and tells the story of a visit by Jesus to America after the Resurrection as well as the history of an ancient tribe of Israelites who settled the Americas six centuries before He was born. Today, the book is interpreted by the Quorum of Twelve and by the church president, who is a living, breathing prophet. These holies are known as "the Brethren" and, to Mormons, they are the highest authority in the world.

A Mormon's lifelong job is to believe and to conform. Every Monday evening, families read together from the Book of Mormon or the Doctrine and Covenants or the Pearl of Great Price. The other six days of the week are carefully regulated. Tuesday nights are for Mutual meetings. Women do their service work on Wednesday nights through the Relief Society. For children, certain nights are given over to Beehive Girls or Gleaner Girls. In high school, there is daily seminary and the Young Adult Group. In church, there is personal testimony: "I believe . . . in the Book of Mormon as the true word of God. I believe . . . in Joseph Smith. That he was a prophet of God."

For an affectionate child, it was a life of warmth and safety. For an intelligent child, it began to require a suspension of disbelief. "When I was about thirteen, I began to question things," Maryann wrote. "Who was this Joseph Smith? Was he a true genius or a lunatic? I began to think there had to be more to life than church all the time and pretty soon I was driving my parents crazy."

Ashamed of the Saints, my own family followed my greatgrandmother to Independence, burning bridges all the way. My father was that mad, grief-stricken woman's grandson, raised to be obedient but also to think. The training in thinking came from his father, who had watched his family disintegrate and who went to law school to compensate. It came from his mother, who was a teacher. And it was something he taught me with all of his might. Never believe in prophets, false or otherwise. Always question. Question everything.

21

I told Maryann that my father had been a lawyer. Too bad he'd died, or he would have rescued her. "He defended the people who couldn't pay," I bragged in one of my letters. "I remember opening the front door to find a basket of tomatoes on the front porch. I remember someone bringing us a freshly caught fish." I pictured Maryann sitting in my father's office. In his red leather chair, which is pushed back a little from his big dark desk, he looks both serious and relaxed. If he is going to represent her, he must know exactly what happened. He must absolutely and emphatically be told every detail. And she must know how to respond to his questions. "If I ask you a question while pulling my handkerchief from my back pocket, understand it to mean that I want you to offer up details. Go overboard. If I use my handkerchief to wipe my brow, show more emotion. Now. What attracted you to William? How did he make you feel?" Between his questions, he turns the chair slightly this way or that to show his displeasure or disbelief or approval. Maryann can see that he is giving her a piece of the future—her future on the witness stand.

"What was it about William?"

She shakes her head. She can still feel the pull of William. She can feel the heat that came off his skin, radiant and confusing. But she says that he was flattering, cheerful, that they got up early in the morning several times a week to play squash.

"Squash?"

"Yes," she says happily. "I like it. It's fun."

My father turns his chair toward the window, which is covered in heavy venetian blinds half-closed. Dust mites litter the air between the blinds and the radiator. He appears to study them. "Did you help him steal your neighbor's gun?"

"No."

"Then how did he know where to find it?" My father stands up, taking his handkerchief out of his pocket as he walks to the window. Through the slats, he can see the sun setting over the buildings that line Kansas Avenue, the gold-green light on flat roofs. He can see the twin steeples of the Catholic church down by the river, where his Mexican clients pray.

Maryann says she has no idea, but my father goes back to his chair, sits down, turns the handkerchief over in his hands and pats his forehead. "Were you and this neighbor friends?" He would like to open the file drawer. It is near his knee on the right side of his desk and it holds his scotch, along with an assortment of other bottles.

"No," says Maryann. "But maybe William got to know him. He was home a lot after he got laid off."

My father pats his brow again. He glares at his pretty client, pushes his handkerchief into his pocket, stands up, pulls his handkerchief out again.

But Maryann is frozen. Maryann is going to evaporate.

22

As our letters became more frequent, I tried to make mine more personal so that Maryann would do the same. I would show her how to study her past, along with the what-ifs. I told Maryann about eloping and running away to Mexico. I told her that Philip had left school and me, and that finding him in Mazatlán five months later felt like a miracle. I'd called an operator in Mexico City and she had tried every beach town and village, finally locating him in a bar, where he had been sleeping every night on a table.

"I miss you."

"So come on down."

"You know I can't do that. My parents would freak. I can't travel with you unless we get married."

I told Maryann that an hour later Philip called again and I traveled from Boulder to Tucson in the backseat of our best friend's father's car. A big convertible. Listening to the radio.

Had a white cotton suit in a white suitcase. My hair up in curlers. "Goin' to the chapel and we're gonna get married . . ."

Still a child.

Maryann wrote back, saying her parents had moved her from Phoenix to Yuma when she was fourteen and that marked the end of her childhood. "Mom and I argued a lot and I stayed gone a lot. Dad would come home and have to play peacemaker. By the way, did I mention I was a daddy's girl?"

She had left her best friend in Phoenix, a girl named Mariann, whom she had met in the sixth grade. "I went to her house a lot cuz she had to keep an eye on her brother and sister while her mom was at work at nights. We went to a nearby mall, Tower Plaza, quite a bit. That's where the skating rink was." Now, at the tender age of fourteen, she began to slip away on weekends, taking a bus back to Phoenix to stay with her friend. Attached like Kahlo's painting of the two Fridas, they were both slender, with long brown hair. "There was a Marie Callender's Restaurant not far from her house. We'd walk over there and get a strawberry pie and she and I would kill it. We would also get a bunch of little kids together—my niece, her niece, some kids we babysat—and have someone drop us off at a local amusement park or the zoo. We had a lot of fun with kids." The other Mariann was serious about church and God and being good, but when they went to the mall to skate, Maryann showed her how to flirt, how to drink and smoke, things she was learning in Yuma. I read this with some surprise. Hadn't she said, in court, that William had introduced her to alcohol and cigarettes? It was there in my yellow notebook. By sixteen, she had a driver's license and drove herself back and forth between Yuma and Phoenix, three hundred miles each way. She swore to herself that she would go back to Phoenix for good as soon as she was done with high school. "Which is exactly what I did," she wrote. "Which is how I met William."

The letters were taking us someplace, but I was asking myself all over again whether, given the drive out to Hanauma

Bay, she might not have pulled the gun on William. ("Stop! Thief! Get out of this car. Joe and I would prefer to go back to the bar and dance!") I was asking myself whether she might not have run out onto a sidewalk in the afternoon sunshine and shouted for help. It was odd. But the more I knew about Maryann, the more I let myself doubt.

Dear Linda,

I didn't consciously think about it at the time, but on some level I knew mom & dad would hate William, which made him all the more attractive. I "needed" to be loved and accepted, to have someone else validate my existence and my worth. As long as I agreed with him, he fulfilled that need. Think Charles Manson and you'll have a good picture of the type of personality William has. I honestly believe, had he been free longer during his life, he would have had a "following." He was a very charismatic, manipulative man. From the time he was 14 until today, and he's 51 now, he's only been free for 14 months of his life. (This little tidbit I found out about after I was arrested.) But in that fourteen months he managed to collect two wives! Today I read his Board Transcripts and realize what an ass he makes of himself; how absurd much of what he says sounds. But back then . . .

Two wives? With the letter, she enclosed an article from *California Legal Magazine*. Its title is "Where Is William Acker?" and it says William is five feet eleven inches tall and weighs 165 pounds. It says his record is closed because he's in the prison witness protection program. But there are a few small disclosures. William was born in Illinois in 1950. His parents split up when he was six months old. His mother remarried twice. The family moved to Paramount, California, when he was two years old and William often ran away. His troubles with the law began when he was six. At fifteen, he was committed to the California Youth Authority. In and out he went, breaking every parole. By 1972, he was in a state prison because of auto theft and burglary. More paroles. More auto thefts, robbery, burglary, and then possession of a firearm. Moved from one prison to another, from one state to another, he's provided information in a dozen cases, including one against Jesse Gonzales, who is now on death row because of William's testimony. Making deals with prosecutors around the country, but especially in L.A., he has created an interesting life for himself. And it all began in 1978, when Bert Bray called the Yuma sheriff's office.

William says he testifies against fellow prisoners in order to bring moral balance to his life. At parole hearings, he maintains that, although he participated in the robberies immediately preceding the murders of Larry Hasker and Cesario Arauza, his wife shot the victims.

Once, however, he told the parole board something different.

23

Parole hearing, William Acker, 1991:

```
COMMISSIONER O'CONNELL:   Okay. What have you
                          discussed in therapy?
         INMATE ACKER:    Well, just about the
                          criminal personality
                          seminar. Basically that
                          criminals want to blame
                          everyone else for their
                          criminal activity. I've
                          done that myself, you
                          know. . . .
            O'CONNELL:    Well, tell me how you've
                          done that then.
               ACKER:     How have I done that?
```

O'CONNELL: Right. How have you changed?

ACKER: Well, I don't make victims of people no more.

O'CONNELL: Okay, then answer me this: Did you commit the murder for which you're in custody?

ACKER: Yes, I did.

O'CONNELL: What about the one in Hawaii?

ACKER: I committed them all and I want the woman behind it, the woman that's incarcerated, I would like her set free.

O'CONNELL: Okay. So Marianne [phonetic] didn't do anything?

ACKER: Absolutely nothing.

O'CONNELL: And is this the first time you've said that?

ACKER: The very first time.

O'CONNELL: Okay. And this is a change of attitude because of this class you took?

ACKER: Listen to me. Marianne Bray [phonetic] has a good family, a family that's willing to help her. Okay?

O'CONNELL: Yes.

ACKER: She's always had that.

O'CONNELL: Yes.

ACKER: Give her that chance.

O'CONNELL: Yes, I'm aware of that. It is difficult, however, to give somebody a parole date when she's sitting there looking at two counts of murder. One of them based solely upon your testimony in Hawaii and the other one, again, based upon your testimony in California.

ACKER: Well the DA's office last board hearing made a real strong point of what I did, you know. In other words, he didn't accept my testimony. So let him stand by that decision. Let him make that decision. Let him make— let that office stand by what they write, what they do, and free that woman. She deserves to be free.

When Maryann read the magazine article in 1992, she sent it to the University of Southern California Wrongful Conviction Project. Would the article help her get paroled? she asked.

One of the law students was about to make a trip to Hawaii. While there, the student telephoned Stephen Hioki, wondering if there were any records of the old trial. Hioki told the student that Hawaii routinely destroyed court transcripts ten years after a trial, but he said that there was something those involved in the USC project should know about Maryann's sentencing—something really important. Judge Au had used the word *accomplice* in his instructions to the jury. And this was improper, Hioki said, because Maryann had not been tried as an accomplice; she'd been tried as the shooter. "At least one jury member said he didn't think she pulled the trigger," Hioki recalled. "So they must have thought the judge gave them permission to find her guilty even if she didn't do it." Hioki said that he had petitioned the court for a judgment of acquittal or a new trial only a month after Maryann was sentenced based on Judge Au's improper instructions. He said the petition was denied. Then he told the USC student that a plea of habeas corpus might be worth trying.

24

That fall, Michael and I were going to spend three months in New York. "Have a safe trip," Maryann wrote. "New York seems like an exciting, yet intimidating city, although I've never been there."

I promised to tell her everything. Seeing things for someone else would be like motherhood all over again: the pleasure of being a conduit. For Maryann, I went to the public library and looked at the vaulted ceilings, marble floors, and rooms that contain the secrets of existence. I went to the Tenement Museum, and the Pierpont Morgan Library, where I saw an exhibit of John Ruskin drawings, manuscripts, and letters. I told Maryann that the Tenement Museum had the kind of apartments that our ancestors probably lived in when they crossed the Atlantic from Europe. I said the Ruskin exhibit cost five dollars to enter and that his work is autobiographical and that he was an only child, whose mother was intensely religious. All through his childhood, I said, she made him memorize sections of the Bible. He was expected to enter the ministry, but instead, he had a breakdown. I said maybe that was what had happened to her, and as I wrote, I imagined Maryann's mother looming over her with the Book of Mormon in hand, telling her to believe it or else.

I told her that up in Times Square a man was living in a block of ice.

In her next letter, Maryann said she knew all about breakdowns. She said during her first years in prison, she had come very close. "I spent many weekends my first couple of years here getting drunk on homemade wine. Most of it's pretty nasty-tasting stuff. But, once you get the first glassful down, you really don't taste the rest. I wasn't dealing with reality very well yet, nor was I being really honest with myself about all that happened. I was very angry with William's betrayal—everything was totally his fault. And I had absolutely no responsibility to bear for any of it."

I kept writing. I told Maryann about the groceries I was buying and how much they cost and what I did with them when I got them home to my rented kitchen. I told her about the movies I was seeing and about an exhibit of photographs taken in the nineteenth century, around the time Ruskin was writing his books and falling in love with a ten-year-old child named Rose la Touche. The photographs were portraits of an Italian contessa, who asked the photographer to lengthen her neck and reduce her waist, as if she could reinvent herself.

Maryann wrote back: "Sometimes I imagine the kind of place I could afford and where I would choose to live and how I would spend my time. I think about the very reduced social life I would have if I got out of here and then about how it would be entirely my own. I mean my life. We women are so new at forging our own identities."

I had no interest in forging a new identity. I was stuck on the past. I told Maryann that it was hard to know whether the Countess Castiglione had created herself or disguised herself in those photographs. I said that if I were locked up the way Maryann was, I'd probably spend all my time trying to re-create my childhood. I'd remember the feel of the carpet on the stairs; I'd remember the smell of the kitchen sink or the dustiness of potatoes in the white metal bin in the dark pantry, where things rarely used were kept. I told her that when my brother was once in the hospital, unable to speak or move, he kept himself sane by recalling our grandparents' house—every inch of it. He began in a corner of the kitchen and made himself remember pictures on the walls, doorknobs, floor surfaces, ceilings, cracks, nails, placement of furniture, saltshakers, dishes, curtains, sounds, smells.

I told her that if I could steal my own life and put it in a glass-topped box, I'd probably do it, then hold it in my hand, run a finger around it. Not because the contents would be beautiful, but because they would be contained, visible, embalmed. Open the box and pick around at the pieces. I said I wished she would do that for me, starting with the house where she lived when she was a child. "A simple description," I said. "Please. Please."

I told her the man who encased himself in ice had reemerged. "Must go to sleep" were his first words. "Can't talk. Can't think."

25

Dear Linda,

My little cell is 8 x 10. As you walk in the door, which has a little window in the middle for the staff to see in, the bunk bed is straight ahead. To the right of the door are two metal lockers and a metal desk with a stool on the left that swings out. To the left of the door is the sink and on the wall around the corner from the sink is the toilet, facing the bunks. Valere—my cell mate—drew a diagram of the room, which I'll enclose. On the wall between the toilet and the bunk are two metal shelves. The bunks, of course, are metal also. Years ago the institution provided wooden lock boxes that we could utilize for storage and they fit perfectly at the foot of the bed. The lid flips all the way back, the opening is toward the mattress, so now it's a shelf and storage, and a good place to write. We are also allowed footlockers, at least for the time being. Valere and I each have one. My tiny TV sits on one. In the past we were allowed to receive personal blankets, sheets, towels, rugs and I've managed to hang on to some things and it helps give the room a better feel. Even though the blanket and bedspread are worn and old, it still helps. I have a latch-hook rug of a wolf on the floor. They are leaning toward making us get rid of all our little comforts which really used to upset and depress me. Now, I just wish they would do what they are going to do and quit messing with us and threatening us. I do like having these little touches of "home," but for a little while longer, I can do without them until I get out and really have a place of my own to call home!

I'm on the top bunk, so I can get up here and kind of be in my own little world. During my lunch breaks during the week, I have the room to myself. It's limited and I'm never just totally by myself, but in my mind I can take myself far away from here. One of my dreams is to, one day, be able to travel. I would love to see Europe like that contessa.

Love ya,
Maryann

26

In January, Michael and I flew home after a snowstorm that smothered New York and after the New Year's Eve celebration, with thousands of people jamming the streets, watching the year 2000 tick away on the Times Square clock. The millennium, when things were supposed to change.

There were no more letters from Maryann.

By March 2001, it was still colder than hell in Toronto (I'm convinced hell is cold) and brutally colorless. March is our famous dog-shit month, when all of it rises to the surface, along with used condoms and the inorganic crap of city life—plastic bags, coffee cups, frozen cigarette butts. I kept telling people about finding Maryann, about writing to her. I found myself referring to her as "my prisoner." It was a terrible phrase but hadn't I put her in prison? Wasn't she my responsibility?

"Don't you care if she's guilty?" people asked.

I said I was trying to find out if I cared. Maybe I had made myself late on that last day of the trial because I wasn't sure. That spring of 2001, we were going to be in California for two weeks. Near Corona. Near the prison. I wrote to Maryann, asking if I could visit. Maybe I was wrestling all over again with what a nice girl like Maryann was doing in a place like that. Or maybe I was trying to find out how much I owed her.

When the last ice disappears and a bit of green emerges, Toronto becomes feverish: deck chairs dragged out of basements, hoses attached to spigots, gardens raked, windows washed. In May, one is glad to have experienced the confinement of winter. Touching the ground, breathing the outside air is bliss. I told myself that the next part of Maryann's life would be like this. She would be sent to Hawaii for the hearing. In my head, I created a vision of her wearing the soft blue muumuu. I saw her unchained, walking through the courthouse, going out through the huge double doors. From the top of the steps, she would look up at the volcanic mountains and beautiful Punchbowl, the extinct volcano under which she once lived. She would adjust her shoulders, unflex her fists. Finally the clock face would crack. Time would begin.

27

I am standing outside a confessional. It's a novelty to me, but apparently I would like to be invited in. I am standing on one foot and then the other, waiting. Go on in! It's time to confess!

But I'm not Catholic!

Never mind about that! The priest will listen to you regardless.

It occurs to me that, in spite of my sins (acts for which I crave forgiveness), what I want to tell the priest is that I've lost my faith. I no longer believe in anything. Perhaps he can offer some advice.

I must say, it's odd to dream so directly from life, since I have indeed felt a sudden draining away of the mystical belief that usually sustains me. There have been times when the sustenance was thin, when I was full of shame and despair. But the shame meant that the faith was still there, lurking. This is different.

I write to Maryann about this dream. I ask her about faith. Does she still have it? Did it leave her and then return, like a lost pet? What about my idea of visiting her?

At last, an envelope arrives. Maryann sends an application for visiting privileges. With it is a list describing the rules for the prison visiting room. It says that the prisoners are allowed to wear one bracelet, one necklace with a charm or religious medallion, one pair of stud earrings, one watch, and two rings. They may not bring in bags or eyeglass cases or cigarette cases or Bibles. They must wear bras and underpants and they may not use the restroom during a visit.

No drinking cups, pens, or umbrellas are allowed. Also no kissing or touching. Embracing may occur when a visitor enters and leaves. No sitting on laps, except for small children. No sitting on the tops of tables or sitting straddled on the bench. No sitting between the legs of visitors.

No mention of faith.

28

The only prisons I have seen are in movies.

This one looks like a big, sprawling brick elementary school. Built for eight hundred women, it holds twice that many and is surrounded by a twenty-foot-high double chain-link steel fence. On top of the fence is a huge roll of razor wire. And around all of this are dairy farms on a scale that is hard to believe. Thousands of dairy cows waiting to be milked, their necks between steel bars.

The waiting room. All those children. Babies in the arms of young fathers. Babies in the arms of grandmothers waiting to visit mothers. And children waiting to visit grandmothers. A family of nine waiting for three hours on the plastic chairs all in a row, the father commanding obedience, not to move, not to wiggle, not to turn and look into the visiting room, where the grandmother would become visible.

It makes me feel faint.

There are no magazines to read. No pictures at which to look. "Do you want me to take you out to the van?" the menacing father asks. "Right now? Do you know what that means?" The old fear hits me: father-fear, and I try to make friends with the children to compensate, to make their daddy see that they are innocents. Then I picture Maryann as she waits for her call. I picture her trying to remember the other side of the steel fence.

There is, first, an outside waiting area. Then the inside waiting room. In the outside area, there are flies. They cover feet and faces and hands as visitors sit in the shade of the concrete-block shelter fanning themselves. But inside we are grim, having passed, one by one, through the metal detector, having put the items we are carrying into a tray and having passed through the electronic gate. We are carrying only a car key, thirty one-dollar bills, and a driver's license in a clear plastic bag. "When's Grammy coming?" The children try to peer through the smudgy glass as their father enforces straight backs and parallel knees. "Do you want to go out to the van?" The baby is thirsty and cries for two hours. There is nothing to drink.

For two hours, we suffer a misery that is a form of penance or a punishment for coming to visit those who are here to be punished. As each prisoner is led into the visiting room, she can be viewed through the dirty glass. Making her way through prisoners and visitors who are shouting and hugging and holding one another, she stops at a line drawn on the floor and waits for the door to be buzzed open, for her mother or sister or husband to cross the line.

I have that picture in my mind of the fragile girl behind big glasses, her soft blond hair, her steady walk, and when I see her cross the crowded room, I know her immediately. She moves as if she is off somewhere else. The hair is short now; the glasses are smaller. She is heavier, harder, but there is that calm, as if all the important questions have already been asked. Then the door is buzzed open and her arms are around me. "It's so good to actually see you." Her hug is fierce.

I am fumbling at my wad of one-dollar bills. No one comes to visit without buying food for the inmate; this much, during the long wait and the observation through glass, has become clear. No inmate comes into the visiting area without being summoned by a visitor and no inmate leaves the visiting area with anything at all—no gift, no souvenir, not even a grain of popcorn. We must consume whatever we buy on the spot. Burritos can be pulled from a machine, carried to the microwave oven, and heated. There are hot drinks, cold drinks, snacks, and ice-cream bars, even fresh fruit. The selection is fantastic.

Maryann is pointing to the buttons, the slot for bills, the place for coins. The prisoners are not allowed to handle money. "Let's go find a seat." Like the other prisoners she's wearing jeans, sneakers, a gray T-shirt. Her rimless glasses are slightly tinted, the kind that darken in sunlight. While I fumble at the slot for change, she retrieves the food and then leads me out to the concrete tables in the open air. We pass the children and their grandmother, who has a warm and intelligent face. "That's Beth. And her best friend. The family always fills out forms for both of them because Gena doesn't get other visitors. It gives her a chance to see someone." Eleven of them around the table, with various board games unfurled, along with cards. Beth and Gena, she says, killed husbands. Most of the lifers are here for that. In this way, she is different. At another table, a little boy's mother and grandmother watch as he runs on the grass. He has spent three hours waiting to get to his mother. Before that, the ride in a hot car, the slicking back of hair, the starchy shirt, while now his mother is distracted. Her eyes are elsewhere.

"It's nothing like prisons in movies, is it?"

I say, "So many older women. Grandmothers. And I can't get over how ordinary everyone looks."

"Any one of us could be your neighbor, right?" Maryann pauses. Then she says, "And you could just as easily be in here."

I stretch out my legs. For several days, I've been worried about this one-on-one conversation with someone I've never met. I've been imagining the awkwardness of wanting to get up and leave. Of being bored. Of running out of talk. Now the first thing I want to say is that I'm stunned by the ugliness of this place; would it be so hard to have a few plants, a few colors, something for the kids besides one set of swings? But that wouldn't be polite. Even if she didn't choose the decor, this is where she has to live. It represents all she has of a public face.

At times like this, people try to establish things they have in common, but all we have is a few days in a Honolulu court-room and the fact that we both got married in Arizona, that I know how it feels to be out on a limb, sawing it off. I could say I recognized some kind of kinship that first day in court, but how much would I be embroidering? I could talk about a night in Guadalajara when Philip's friend Roberto pulled a gun on a stranger who asked me to dance. I was twenty years old and it was thrilling.

The California Institution for Women is run by the state. Maryann says it was built to look like a campus back in the 1950s, when the brick housing units were called "cottages" and each woman had a cell to herself. But when Ronald Reagan became governor of California, the cells got double- and triple-bunked. Beds were put in the auditorium and the gym. Programs were cut. Now lifers are told that any trouble will get them shipped north, to a tougher place. "The new prisons are so much worse." While Maryann explains this, she's giving me time to get my bearings. We have our food spread out on our laps, and she's saying that CIW has two kinds of inmates. The drug users are Level 2s. "Parole breakers. Things like that. They come in, go out, screw up, come back in again. They're stupid. They have a chance and they blow it." She shakes her head in a show of disgust. The lifers, she says, don't mix with the Level 2s. Like everywhere else, there is a hierarchy here. Maryann and the other lifers are Level 4s. And they are allowed a little more leeway. "But no conjugal visits. The men ruined that for us. Male prisoners, I mean."

"How so?"

"Well, their women got pregnant, then had to go on welfare."

"So this is the only kind of visit allowed."

"But in the old days, we could have a whole weekend in a special house. With our family or husband. But not now."

"Your folks used to come?"

She nods. "Every chance they got. And when they couldn't drive, a few times my sister brought them. Then my mom died from cancer four years ago, and after that Dad didn't give a rip anymore. I lost him this past July, the day before his eighty-fourth birthday."

"Are you and your sister close?"

"She won't take my calls. They run up her phone bill. When I was adopted, she just never got over it. The one I loved was Polly. Pauline. She was my Navajo foster sister. Now I don't know where she is."

"You were adopted?" At last maybe I am on to something.

"I never told you? It's a short, short story."

It is an afternoon in January 1960 and a clerk at the county courthouse in Phoenix decides not to take her lunch break. Everyone else has left the building, but she wants to catch up on the work that's been piling up. She's rummaging through a stack of papers next to the phone when a man comes through the door, panting, out of breath. He's come up the stairs at a run. He wipes his hands on his trousers. "Where do I adopt a baby?" he blurts out.

"You want a baby?"

"No, ma'am. I already have one. Or rather, my son does. Or rather, my stepson. Does."

The clerk studies the man. He's young, in his early forties, and he's wearing work clothes. "Where is this baby?" she asks softly, so as not to frighten him, and meanwhile she reaches across the pile of papers and edges the heavy telephone closer to her chair. She has not stood up or changed the look on her face, which is calm and businesslike.

"At its mother's . . ." He shakes his head. "But that's no problem, ma'am, believe you me."

The clerk has the number in her head. "Just a sec. Maybe I can help." Her friend Gladys. And Bert. Lost their boy just two months ago to an asthma attack. She feels no need to explain herself. All her work at the courthouse, all her work for the church, all her life has taught her to think of the greater need. No reason to explain that their first baby died and now they've lost the boy—it's nobody's business, and anyway the phone is ringing. "Gladys! Get Bert quick. I have a baby for you!" The clerk covers the receiver with her hand and whispers, "I forgot to ask. Girl or boy?" Then, taking her hand away, she shouts, "No kidding! I mean it. Get Bert right over here this minute." Now Maryann looks at me. "That's the way it begins," she says, "my story. In a courthouse."

We sit there for a long, long minute. "It must have been hard for Penne."

Maryann nods. "I can see that now. She loved her brother and he just died, and suddenly there's this baby being spoiled and getting all the limelight. All through the years, we've had terrible fights. The last one was the last time the family came up to stay here with me. Penne kept saying, 'My mom' this and 'My mom' that, and I finally blew up at her and told her she'd been doing that to me all my life. I told her, 'She's my mom, too!'"

"Were they overly protective, your parents?"

"I was cherished. I know that."

"Except for your sister."

"Well, she was attached to her brother, who died." She looks away. "Do you have a sister?"

I say no. I say my brother died ten years ago. Crashed his plane and killed himself and his second wife. I say it was an accident. Then I think of the grief that seems to multiply—ripples and ripples of grief—and for a minute I can see the tail of something disappear just around the corner of my mind. A brother and sister in Hawaii . . . I want to call it back, but Maryann is saying that her parents just wanted her to marry a good person and have a good life. Because everything, or almost everything, had already happened to this family long before Maryann met William. Two brothers had died, one as an infant, one at the age of fourteen. After that, Penne collected boyfriends, got pregnant, married outside the faith, outside the race. Because of Penne's love for a black man, the whole family was shunned. "Can you imagine what that's like? Nobody talks to you or even looks at you. It was hard hard on my mom. Her own father was terrible to us. Her whole family was. After that, we never saw much of them."

"No wonder you started to question the church."

"After Penne, everyone said it was up to me to make things right. But I was running around behind their backs. I was giving my parents the blues before I hit sixteen. Mom actually loved my first boyfriend. He was what she wanted for me."

"Before William."

"I mentioned Doug in a letter. Remember? Returned missionary. Six two. Sandy hair. Good-looking. He was the reason I moved back to Phoenix from Yuma as soon as I got out of high school. Well, which I wanted to do anyway, I guess. But just think. If I'd adhered to the teachings of chastity, morality, and faithfulness . . . who knows? If I hadn't rebelled against religion, I never would have given William the time of day. Even when I met him, I was still active in the church. If Doug hadn't gone out of town for eight weeks with his job, I wouldn't have been looking for someone else to amuse myself with. I wasn't very faithful to that man. But when he was in town, things were great. We probably would have ended up getting married, but I met and married William during this extended business trip. Met him and married him before Doug even came back. Like that"—snapping her fingers—"I really wasn't thinking seriously of getting married at eighteen. I still wanted to live my life." She stops talking and listens, as if there is another conversation going on in her head, a conversation of real what-ifs. In Phoenix, the landlady had a sofa. Maryann had brought her water bed from home and she built a new frame for it. She got dressed in the morning and went to work at Arizona Hardware, the same distribution company that employed her father. At work, she was pleasant to people, and when a co-worker mentioned a brother who was coming to stay, Maryann showed polite interest. "She said he'd had a rough life. She said he was a sweet guy who needed someone to care about him."

Doug was away on that business trip.

And William got a job working for Arizona Hardware, in the warehouse. One day he came inside and met Maryann. It was after lunch, sometime in the afternoon. He was sweating a little. He had the look of something abandoned, like the kitten she had taken in a few weeks before. He had a mother in California. And the sister. But he was just out of jail and he talked a blue streak. "At eighteen, I wasn't thinking about who this guy is. . . ." They went out the evening of the day they met and then he came back to her place, as if he belonged to her. Like the lost cat. He needed her. There had always been expectations from men, always, but never like this. The way he came straight at her. He didn't know any better than that. He wasn't experienced. It was what she thought about. Helping him. The way he reached out to touch her to prove something to himself. The way his future was up to her. He liked to drink, unlike Doug, but for Maryann it was a daytime/nighttime shift, two sides of herself, light and dark. "Bill was so exciting to be with. It wasn't like anything I'd ever experienced ever, being with him."

She was living back in Ward Fourteen, where she'd grown up, where everyone knew her. The old neighbors talked her into coming back to teach Sunday school. They wanted her to run the Young Adult Group. So she was living two lives. Going to work, going to church. Then rushing off to William.

"My kitten refused to be in the same room with Bill. Whenever he came home, the kitten hid, ran to a closet or under the bed. I should have paid attention. The kitten was right. Once, it jumped down from the window over the bed and bit him hard. He had taken a shower and was lying there naked. He screamed. That kitten bit him in the balls." Maryann grinned.

Within days of moving in, William was talking marriage. "He kept bugging me about it, and then he caught me one day when I just said, 'Yeah, okay,' just to shut him up. But the next thing I knew, I was calling my parents."

While she's telling me this, I remember William on the witness stand saying, "We got married a month after we met. Oh, Maryann could play emotional games, man. She was able to tap on emotions pretty good." So I look at her. The room around us is still bright with noise and chaos, but I shut it out. How much do I believe? How much of our brand-new friendship is concocted out of thin air and guilt?

29

One afternoon, Maryann's best friend—the one named Mariann—dropped by the apartment and went home in tears. It was a defining moment. It was the moment Maryann made a choice. She was forsaking her best friend, someone she'd loved since they were eleven years old. She was forsaking this twin because William was drinking beer and saying religion was a crutch. When he asked Mariann what she believed in, she started talking about Joseph Smith, and William snarled. He said Mormons were lame and weak-minded, that they should learn natural principles. "Nothing worse," he said, "than holding an idea in your head with zero evidence." After he said that, he squashed up his beer can and threw it across the room, which made Maryann mad, but what could she do? He said the law of nature was obvious, and he was pointing at the plate-glass window as if it framed the universe. "You people do group-think," he told Mariann, and he lay down on the landlady's sofa and covered his face with one bent arm and talked about Ayn Rand and self-interest. Self-interest instead of self-denial. "That leads to freedom," he said.

Mariann knew he was out on parole. But she didn't mention that; she was too polite. At church, they said you know what's true because you can feel it. She said, "Evaluating shows a lack of faith."

"That's the kind of bullshit they teach you. Along with some lie about Joseph Smith!" William snorted. He sat up and glared at her as if everything in the world were her fault, as if her stupidity had put him in jail. "I'm not into the false," he told her. He was getting drunk. The can he'd thrown across the room was his sixth or seventh beer in two hours. Wasn't it true that little kids gave testimony about things they couldn't know? Wasn't that a form of brainwashing? Mariann said, "Giving testimony produces the knowing."

Maryann looked at her friend. They both knew that arguing with boys was part of a game. It was a little seductive. They'd both listened to plenty of wild ideas. It was possible that their parents and teachers and even the elders were wrong. Even the bishop. It was possible that William could answer the secret questioning in her heart. When he said that self-interest is actually a virtue, it made her understand something, because she'd watched her mother bend and scrape for everyone else. She'd admired her mother, but William was right when he said if you take care of your own needs, you do a better job of everything else, because she could never be like her mother; she knew that; and maybe charity is unnatural. Her mother scrubbing that little girl who had lice when her family moved into the neighborhood. Are animals charitable? Tigers? Birds? Humans aren't animals, but isn't nature part of a human being? Mariann was arguing with William about how God set humans apart, and when William laughed, Maryann saw her wipe her face with the heel of her hand and turn away. She noticed when her friend put down her beer, placing it carefully on a coaster the way she always did. She heard Mariann say she was going home and she should have crossed the room then and said something nice, but when her friend left, even then, she didn't run after her or call the next day, because William needed her and a true friend should know what that means. Need creates duty, but to choose between a friend and a lover was the hardest thing in the world. She had to remind herself that hard things are strengthening.

The next day, she told William that he could try hypnotizing her. He had been promising he could do it, so maybe he could. And she had nothing to hide. While Maryann admitted this much, I let myself add details. They sat on the floor in the bedroom and pulled down the shades. I could almost see them with my own eyes, sitting face-to-face, William holding his knife up in front of her. And she must have felt a kind of interesting chill. Then William tells her to watch the knife, keep her eyes on it and let herself go. "Like doing it," he says. "Just relax." He's moving the knife back and forth close up to her face, saying Justice can defend against evil. He calls his knife Justice, and Maryann thinks back to the day she'd gone out to buy it, how he had sent her off to the store for an eight-inch Buck knife. He sent her to buy it because he was on parole, and she went in and purchased the best knife they had in the store, and it felt perfect giving him something he wanted when he didn't have anything else. She gave it to him like a present and he asked her to carry it for him because it sealed them. Like in a ceremony. At the temple. When Mormons seal something, it's for life. Maybe it's strange to name a knife, but William doesn't have anything else to name. Not a pet. Not a home or a car or the things that matter to men who are twenty-eight. From now on, she's going to go along with him instead of arguing about every little thing, because trust is important. Even if she doesn't necessarily believe what he's saying, it helps him to stay calm; it keeps his understandable insecurities at bay. Ayn Rand worshipped the great and the exceptional, never the underdog. And look at William. He already has a following, a network of Randanians. He talks to them. He gets messages all the time. People believe in him and send him messages and look after him. And now, with her help, he can go someplace. "Did you know why he was in jail?" I asked, breaking in on my own thoughts.

"He said it was all a misunderstanding about a gun," Maryann said, then, a little abruptly, "Do you want something more to eat?"

For a brief moment, I see Philip's friend Roberto putting his hand into his back pocket. I hear his little gun tap the underside of the table at the dance bar in Guadalajara. Why had he come on my honeymoon? How had he gotten to be part of my life? It was a big dance bar and I was wearing a full-skirted, backless black dress with white polka dots. I felt both newly married and sexy, although that feeling did not last through the summer. "Okay, sure." I pick up the plastic bag with the money, my car key, my driver's license, thinking another coffee would be welcome. I'm really tired. I need a break. It would be comforting to watch the paper cup drop down inside the vending machine and the coffee dribble into the cup. There are moments that bring me close to paralysis, when I start thinking of a particular time that might have gone another way.

"I remember the night the neighbors were burglarized," Maryann said as we crossed the floor. She often uses legal-sounding language, as if she reads arrest warrants at night to put herself to sleep. "I came home and there was a police car in the driveway and William was out taking a walk. I found out after we got to Hawaii, the first time he pulled the gun on me, that he was the one that had robbed my neighbor."

But hadn't she said in court that she knew he was traveling with a gun when they left Phoenix? I thought about asking but then decided against it. I was too tired to make sense of anything.

"Anyway," she said as I was sliding a dollar into the coffee machine, "the trip was going to be a delayed honeymoon. Bill made it sound romantic."

"Was it?"

"I remember getting off the plane and the air hitting us, all the humidity and the smell of flowers, and already, within a few minutes, William started to seem different. I don't know what it was. When we first got there . . . before everything got totally insane, we took the bus out to Hanauma. I remember that. It was spectacular. The clearness of the water. The lushness of the hills. My memories aren't all bad about that place."

I said yes, but I said it in a distracted kind of way because I was remembering how it felt to have my face in the salty water of that bay. I was remembering how my brother taught me to use a snorkel, adamant about the pleasure of seeing things from underneath. I'm fourteen years old and I've come out to Hawaii from Kansas, first driving with my parents to California and then getting on a plane for the first time. Maybe Skip wanted to rescue me and maybe he almost did. What I remember about that island is the air: temperature, moisture, smell. And the nights. They were so intense, I can hardly think of them now.

"We climbed around and explored some of the caves. It was like we were just a normal couple. And we were actually still up there when they cleared the beach that evening. Everyone left and we ended up camping up there. I remember after all the people cleared out, watching a mongoose come out and play on the beach."

"It sounds . . ." I was thinking, Unbelievable, but again a picture, unbidden, formed in my mind. A mongoose, long and thin and sly, peers out from behind a rock, checking for safety, its head moving in suspicious jerks. Maryann is carrying the little Kodak her parents gave her for Christmas. She's watching William watch the animal, putting the camera in front of her face. She's thinking this is what honeymoons are supposed to be. Something to keep in an album, something to remember and look back on in life.

30

That spring, I would visit the prison three times. I was on the right side of the mirror: That's how it felt, surrounded by something familiar, something left over from the phone calls my father used to take while we sat at the dinner table. The phone was so close that we listened, my mother and I, wondering what was being said on the other end of the line. After dinner, my father would take a short nap and then go back to the office. On Saturdays, he was at the office. On Sundays, he was at the office after lunch. And there were those summers when I went to the courthouse with files and ran errands and answered the office phone with a list of the law partners' names.

Around my father, always, there was a sense that without his immediate attention, matters of importance would fall apart. Wherever he went, my father's briefcase was bulging with work that was overdue. Once, I was taken to the office on a Saturday, when there was no one else around. A couple arrived, not especially young. She was wearing a dark coat and a head scarf tied under her chin. He was carrying his hat, as was proper at the time. My father went out to the hall and came back with a baby, very pink and wrapped up. Young as I was, maybe ten or eleven at that time, I was given the baby to give to the woman in the head scarf. She put out her hands and I handed the baby over. She was wearing red lipstick and she thanked me. As if I'd arranged it. As if I'd given that baby away myself.

So, I went back to the prison, wearing my father's shoes. On my second visit, I was kept waiting outside for several hours. A man who appeared to be ill or exhausted sat outside in the shelter with me. "My sister's in there," he told me, running a hand over his shaved head. "She has six months to live." Across from us was the high double fence with its razor wire. "We had a lawsuit. Because of the bad medical care." I had to listen hard to catch all the sorrow. The wind was blowing dirt and trash. A woman was sent home to get her baby's birth certificate, which must have a state seal affixed, which cannot be a copy like the one she had brought, although she and the baby come every week. The drive home takes an hour. An hour back.

After an hour of waiting, I wandered across the dirt path to the fence. I could see Maryann sitting outside with the Mormon woman Sheron, who had been assigned by the church to visit her on a regular basis many years before. She had become Maryann's determined friend. Now I shouted to them that I had not been approved yet to come in. Maryann's friend Sheron made a frantic "Go away" motion with her hands just as a loudspeaker blared at me to get back across the road. "She's a good girl," Sheron said sternly, grabbing my arm, when I finally got into the visiting room. "Never gets in trouble, and because of you, the guard gives her a warning."

Next came the rush to the vending machines, as if they were gods to be pacified. The woman with cancer? "That's

Sherrie. Been here since the eighties. She's had mastectomies, chemotherapy, radiation, but they won't let her out." We were sitting like friends with our soft drinks between us, Sheron having left as I arrived. Now I heard about the wedding and the parents: how Maryann's mother cried on the phone and how both mother and father drove up to Phoenix from Yuma. Her father brought a friend. The two older men came into the apartment to talk to William while Maryann went out with her mother to sit in the car. "Are you getting married because you have to?" I remembered my own mother's words: "And just who is it that you're marrying?" I remembered her reaction. I was running away. Really escaping. I remembered the way she arranged for a cake, flowers, champagne. In Tucson. In spite of everything.

In Phoenix, in the tiny apartment, no one budged. The men talked for an hour and then left. But in the morning, Maryann's father called and said they were still in town. They had not gone home. "I'm going to put Mother on."

"Do you have flowers?" she asked. "What do you need?"

Maryann would be married by the bishop in a room off to the side of a church. It would not be the temple wedding of her dreams. She'd wear a wedding dress that William had chosen, and after the ceremony he'd call her "Mrs. Acker" several times to her face.

"That bothered me. I didn't like it."

The good, steady boyfriend off on a business trip.

On her wedding night, back in her apartment, she sat down by the phone. "I remember that so clearly. We'd been drinking since morning. Bill went to bed. I sat out in the living room by the phone. I had this sudden desire to call Doug. But it was too late. That was the minute I knew I had made a mistake." She looked at me intently. It is a way she has of looking—both intent and passive. "You know, I was raised that marriage is forever, that you follow your husband. Obedience."

I saw myself crossing the border with Philip, giving my life away. "You ride in the back," my new husband says, and I climb in with my girlish white suitcase. His friend Roberto is waiting for us on the other side of the Rio Grande. It's a potent moment, sitting there in the back of a car so dear to me that I used to see it in my dreams. There are Coke bottles and beer bottles and pieces of paper floating around. The smell of old cigarettes. The kittenish sound of the engine as Philip and Roberto chatter away in Spanish and I am swallowed by the dustiest of highways.

Maryann said she was drinking excessively all that day. That's the word she used, *excessively*. "William drove out to a friend's house to borrow a jacket and got lost on the way back. The wedding was at five in the evening. I spent the day running errands and drinking. When I got to the church at four-thirty, my parents were already there, along with a few guests. Mom was in the church kitchen making a frappé for the reception, saying she only wanted my happiness. She said that if William made me happy, that was enough, but she asked if I wanted to think things through a little longer. Shouldn't I take more time? Then I remember being in the bathroom with my best friend and her asking me if I was sure about getting married to William. I probably said something like: Once you get to know him and understand him . . . And I remember standing in front of the bishop. I didn't walk down the aisle with Dad. We were all just sitting in the room; then the bishop came in, we stood up, and he married us. Then we had the little reception, where William would only call me Mrs. Acker."

At the reception, people mingled as if the sudden marriage had been a foreseeable event, someone taking pictures, everyone talking. And then it was over, bride and groom taking off to Sizzler for dinner, the parents driving home to Yuma. Back in the apartment, the groom went to bed and the bride found herself in the dark living room.

I had told her I'd gotten married in Arizona. Mentioned the champagne and the cake and the motel with its cactus lit up by the spotlight at the heart of the night. I was still looking for links, but, sitting there with her, I forgot to imagine what it would be like to have no horizon, no sense of context, not to know where the next town is or how big the Alta Dena Dairy is next door, with all those black-and-white cows living without injury or joy.

31

On the third visit, she tells me about finding her father. "Biological," she calls him. A father hears from the child he gave away when she was two months old. She's calling from prison, where she has spent all her adult life. A counselor has helped her locate him and she has asked another inmate to write to him because "what if he wanted nothing to do with me? I didn't want to just barge in on his life."

"And your mother, your birth mother?"

"I'm not interested. She's not someone I need to meet."

"Because of being adopted?"

"No, being adopted was fine. I was chosen. I always knew that. It was the best thing to be. It's just that I know what we have in common. She was wild. She was only sixteen when she had me and she already had a three-year-old. Pretty obviously, my good side comes from my adopted parents, and I know where the other part comes from. I know about nature and nurture. They teach that in here."

"But do you know her name?"

"The thing is, there's so much I have to think about and concentrate on and get done. I have to work on my parole."

I'm looking around at the huge, bleak room we're sitting in. It's enough to drive me crazy, all this gray concrete and the row of twinkling vending machines. On one sorry wall, there is a glass case full of baby blankets and small trinkets the prisoners have made. These are for sale, but I have never seen anyone spend so much as a second looking at them. There is, of course, nothing to read. Except the Bible. There is a guard near the door, talking on the phone. She is female, but that isn't saying anything. Maryann turns to smile at someone. "Maria. Born in a little village in Mexico and ends up in this place."

I say, "You know while I'm here, I thought we could talk about what really happened in Hawaii. We've never talked about that."

She's still looking at Maria. No change in the eyes or face. "You heard my testimony." It isn't a question. "At first, I wouldn't even admit things to myself. Not even that I was present. Not even to my attorney." Then she goes back to Maria, saying she came up with her father when she was sixteen. As if she is answering my question, she says the village where Maria was born had no electricity and no running water, but up here she was more or less abducted by a woman who offered her a job, telling her not to tell her family, to keep it for a surprise. Maria was driven straight to an old man's house off in the hills, far from anything she recognized, and the old man told Maria he was a *brujo*. For five long years, he raped her and beat her, although Maryann tells this part without emphasis. When somebody killed the old man, Maria was blamed. Maryann opens her hands and looks at her nails, while I remember the test we used as girls to see if we were feminine. Open or closed hands. "She gets angry about how naïve she was, but considering the environment in which she was raised, it's understandable, don't you think?"

I say, "And you went off with William for the same reason."

"What do you mean by that?"

"I mean you were brought up to believe in male authority. Prophets. Doctrines of faith. If Joseph Smith could establish brand-new rules a hundred years ago, why couldn't William Acker do it today?"

Maryann shakes her head. "No. It wasn't that. I truly believed he had a network that would hurt me or my family." She shakes her head again. "I did what he said. It wasn't belief; it was fear. And I was right. When I finally came to my senses and told him to go to hell, that's when he made his first statement about Hawaii in L.A. and started his revenge."

"But, Maryann, in the beginning. That's what I'm talking about."

"Middle-class people, most people can't understand the feeling I had with William. Most people have never felt like that."

"I'm not so sure."

"Well, you have, but it's not usual. He was different from anyone else. Really different. He was an ex-con, the tattoos, everything. I was eighteen. I was horny. I knew Mom and Dad would never approve. That was huge. And in the beginning, he stoked my ego, sure. He was exciting, dangerous. I wanted to prove my independence at all costs. And the cost has been unbelievable. The Doug, the picket fence, and the two-point-five kids or two-point-eight or whatever . . . I wanted nothing to do with that. I would not conform. That was the big appeal. I'd never met anyone like William."

"So it wasn't fear. Not at first. Then in Hawaii he started being different."

"I still loved him. I was crazy for him. It doesn't make any sense. Even in Phoenix, I should have known better. There were signs. One time, he saw some man in a car stop and talk to me as I was walking down the street going to the store. Never happened!" She looks down and notices her food, touching it gingerly. "Then in Hawaii . . . one night he went out and I stayed in the apartment and sometime in the middle of the night I felt him grabbing me, yelling about who the man was that just left the apartment." Maryann's face is not easy to read. "He was drunk, but he swore he hadn't been drinking. He swore he saw a man walk out of our apartment and as they passed on the outside stairs, William asked him what he was doing. The man said he'd been in 'Maryann's apartment.' I've heard about people with chemical reactions to alcohol that go way beyond being drunk. Or maybe he was putting on quite the act. Anyway, I had to do some fast thinking and talking to get him to calm down. And the next day when he saw the bruises on my arm and shoulder from where he'd grabbed me, he didn't have a clue where they came from."

"We were going to talk about the crimes," I say, looking over at the clock, because I have to leave in an hour. I push my chair back and lean forward to show Maryann that I am here as a friend, that my friendship is serious, but I live in Canada, and who knows if I'll ever be back? The metal legs of the chair make a scraping sound on the bare concrete.

"When William turned himself in, you know, he said he was going to cut me loose," she says dreamily. "He said I had nothing to worry about; he wasn't going to let me take the fall. And I was in jail, so instead of cooperating with the detectives, I kept up with the lies he had drilled into my head. To make matters worse, I had a lawyer for the California trial who had never done defense." She forces a laugh. "He was actually a prosecutor that got assigned to my case."

We aren't talking about the crimes; we're talking about William again.

"Before the California trial, we were offered a deal by the DA. They would have me plead guilty only to robbery if William would plead guilty to the murder. So, I walked out with William telling me to think about it, and when we went into the courtroom a little later, I said, 'Take the deal,' and he started yelling at me. He called me a bitch and went off in front of the judge, and my attorney requested that our trials be severed. The judge made me waive my rights to a jury trial because he needed a conviction for his own separate reasons. He was Mormon, which is funny. He was being investigated for making pornographic phone calls. So I was convicted by that judge under the felony murder rule, and within a month William made his first statement about the Hawaii case, blaming me, saying I was the only shooter. He had pleaded no contest to Cesario Arauza's murder and he still hadn't been sentenced. So maybe he thought it would help his case. If he came up with a present for them, they'd be more lenient. That's how William works. I hadn't spoken or written to him since the fight in court, so next he cut a deal to testify against me in Hawaii in exchange for immunity. I really never dreamed he would go to such extremes. And when he did, I didn't believe anything could possibly come of it; they couldn't use my husband's testimony against me."

"But they changed the law."

"The prosecutor had no case against me without William is why."

"Did you know that the DA's son was killed the same way? Maybe he thought the murders were connected. He needed to find Larry Hasker's killer." We have been sitting with our food uneaten. We have been talking as if there is no time limit, no bell that will ring or lights that will flash. Now Maryann looks down at her food again, and I wonder if she's waiting for me to eat first, the way people wait for the hostess at a dinner party.

"At times, I think he may have set me up when he sent me out for cigarettes on that last night," she says quietly, still not moving. "But then, why would he turn himself in? That night when he gave me the car keys and twenty dollars, my only thought was, This is my chance to get away! Then I only got a couple blocks when I got pulled over."

I'm about to bite down on the tortilla and beans, still vaguely warm. No crimes. Only the aftermath. Added to which, the lights are flashing. The count. It takes place in the middle of visiting hours, another humiliation, since the women who have visitors are separated from them and have to line up outside for an hour or more. Visitors stay on the benches close to the vending machines, talking to one another, trying to keep children amused. Every inmate in every prison in California is being counted. On my first visit, this happened while I was still in the waiting area, and it made the waiting that much longer. There is no leaving, either. Once the count starts, doors are on lockdown. On this, my third visit, I have waited an hour and fifteen minutes to see Maryann. Finally, I'm inside. We've been talking for less than thirty minutes and now the lights flick off and on.

"Shit. I can't wait here for another whole hour to talk, Maryann. Michael and I are going to something in La Jolla. I have to drive back." I'm actually embarrassed to admit that I have a life.

Maryann stands up as if I've pushed her. "I was completely under his influence," she insists, while the narrow bench is between us and people around us are beginning to stir. "Mentally and emotionally. But afterward, when we got caught, I had to finally do something, which was to finally tell the truth and pray that you on the jury found more in my testimony that fit the physical evidence." She looks straight at me. "Although unfortunately, the truth didn't matter. Someone had to pay. That's what one of them said. Remember?"

"In my notebook I have a quote that goes something like 'If you think she pulled the trigger and did so with intent, then you must find her guilty.' Was that the judge instructing the jury? Or was it Hioki?"

"Yeah, I think that was my guy. Anyway, one of the jurors said they didn't necessarily believe that I pulled the trigger, but they couldn't let a crime of that magnitude go unpunished."

"If Judge Au said something else, though, like, 'If you think she was present and participating in the event, then you must find her guilty,' if he said that, they'd have had no choice."

"It's not the law in Hawaii. But I guess he said it. Do you know, when they came back after only forty-five minutes and found me guilty on all charges, I went numb from the inside out. My knees buckled just the way you read about. I didn't understand how they could have possibly believed William's lies."

"It was an hour and forty-five minutes." And Judge Au had used the word *accomplice*, whether it was the law in Hawaii or not. I'm beginning to think that there is nothing to be won. Not anymore. Maybe there is no point in pondering the what-ifs. But I try one more question. "When did you find out about your mother?"

"I was fourteen or so."

"And that was exactly when you started getting wild." We have not even opened our popcorn, but the food will have to be left uneaten. Without a visitor, she will have to hurry back to her cell, since she can no longer be in the visiting room.

She smiles. "Linda, I can't say for sure what brought you back into my life at this point, but we have a unique bond, wouldn't you say?" And while the prisoners begin to line up outside, she hugs me. "Linda . . . after so many strange turns, I can't help thinking suspiciously. I instantly began wondering about the woman in the prosecutor's office without even knowing what was said. I think she could have carried your comment about not being sure of my guilt back to the office. Your being a few minutes late could have just been very convenient to their wants. Most people wouldn't think along those lines," Maryann continues, glancing up at the clock, "but there were too many things in Hawaii that just didn't add up until I found out about

William's plea bargain. Like, a good lawyer was removed as my counsel and replaced by Hioki." She sighs. "I had him put in a motion to withdraw from my case, but the judge denied it."

We are edging toward the door, stowing our trash. We pass the grandmothers and the mothers being visited. We pass the grandmothers and the mothers visiting. And the children. And the men. I glance at Maria and at the faces of two or three hundred other prisoners. Less than a month before, fourteen dehydrated Mexicans had died near Yuma. Another thirteen barely survived. They'd been wandering for a week in 114-degree heat after being dumped by the "coyotes" who brought them across the Rio Grande to get to a better life.

had told her to call. She would have to do that collect.

I transcribed some of the pages of the yellow notebook and sent them to her, even the page where I called her a sullen, brutal bitch. I said that maybe together we could try to tell her story.

She didn't call.

What did I expect?

When she finally wrote, she said she remembered the man who couldn't be objective because he thought anyone who carried a gun must intend to use it. She said she remembered the blue muumuu but not the white dress. Then she said that for seven months, in jail in Hawaii, they'd come into her cell every fifteen minutes all night long and shine a light in her eyes. "I was on a suicide watch. I learned on the plane going over that William made a bargain with the state, but I wasn't about to kill myself. I'm not the type. Still, when I read your initial thoughts of me in the courtroom . . . the image I portrayed to the jury, I thought, 'No wonder they convicted me!' I truly must have appeared to be that cold-blooded bitch. If I had not been keeping such a tight rein on my emotions . . . but there was so much going on inside me and I was so afraid of what would happen if I let even a crack in that wall. I would drown in the flood. But of course none of you had a clue to that because of my tight grip. Would the outcome have been different if I'd broken down? And of course I wasn't prepared at all by Hioki to take the stand. And I thought the truth would be enough. Silly me!" She said that her mother wasn't there in the courtroom, that I was right about that.

I went to see my own mother and attended my high school reunion. Two weeks later, when I was back in the house on the river, back in Canada, I got a message that Maryann had called and would call again. At last. But what would we talk about? I thought I could tell her about the reunion. I would turn it into a story, the way I used to turn my life into stories for my mother. It was the way I kept things on track in our house. I'd tell Maryann I had flown down to Topeka and settled in at my mother's right away. I'd tell her that settling in involves taking my bag into the guest room, sniffing and poking at things, then sitting down at the dining room table for a glass of iced tea and some cookies. At this point in the visit, we are both shy, I'd say. Only this time, my mother had not greeted me at the door. She had not gone into the kitchen for tea while I put my bags down. She was in bed when I arrived, and I went to her room and she batted her hand in the dark air around her head. No book in her hand. No television or radio. No interest in me.

The high school reunion took place at a big new hotel on the fairgrounds. We had a Kansas City band, and after two glasses of wine, I got into the spirit. The boy I'd had a crush on all through junior high had a white mustache now. His mother had Alzheimer's, and he gave me the name of the place where she lived, but I wasn't paying much attention. Those Topeka boys can dance. I learned with them, and we do the same thing on the floor, unlike any other partners I've had. For one of those dancers, I'd once had a secret name. He'd married his high school sweetheart after leaving a first wife, running away to Hawaii, sailing off to the South Pacific. For Maryann, I would make all this appealing.

What do we make of ourselves and how much is circumstance? When I was eighteen, I graduated from high school and left home for college. Never wrote to my friends. Burned the first bridge. What a potent year that first one away from home can be; it decides everything. Now I sat at the river's edge, wondering how to tell Maryann the story. I'd tell her that one measures one's changes at such times. "This is what it will be like for you," I'd say. "Every step beyond the prison gate will be a contrast with yourself at eighteen."

But when the call finally came through, she didn't ask about the reunion. She asked about my mother. She sounded worried. I said I couldn't talk about it. I said something about going home, that it was hard. I had walked two blocks to see my old house, the one where I grew up. Crossed the park and stood there seeing my parents through the windows, young again, my father pounding the table, out of breath. I said, "I used to tell my mother stories. But I think she's maybe past listening." Late night and I am upstairs in my room. My father is back at the office, although earlier he and my mother had highballs in the kitchen—he, sitting on the yellow step stool with the evening paper, and she, dancing between sink and fridge and stove. She had taken her bath, unpinned her hair, put on high heels. He would be home for an hour. For an hour, things would be sexually charged between them. Then it is night and she is downstairs watching television. She is downstairs alone and I am alone upstairs.

"Want to hear the story of my second marriage?"

"What?"

Was Maryann trying to cheer me up? It was a reversal of roles, but I listened. She said she and William were already divorced at the time of the trial in Hawaii, and when she came back to prison in California, she started writing to a pen pal—Robert. First he wrote; then he got approved as a visitor; then he proposed to her. It all happened in six months—another whirlwind courtship—but, as Maryann put it, why would any sane person want to marry someone in prison? She was working as a clerk for her counselor and asked him about the proposal. Asked her parents, too. And if it now seems unreasonable to imagine sustaining a marriage under such a bizarre circumstance, I have to remember that she longed for a shred of the outside world in an otherwise-shattered life, someone to care about her, to visit her, to look after her emotionally. "What do you have to lose?" the counselor asked. Her sentence would not go on forever. She would be out in a few years. "Women were actually being paroled in those days. Lifers. Not like now." Maybe the conviction in Hawaii would not have great consequence. Hioki was going to appeal because of Judge Au's instruction to the jury.

A year after the Hawaii case wrapped up, she married Robert in a small room in a corner of the administration building. Her parents were there—a second wedding to be witnessed. Robert's brother and a sister came along and there were five or six inmates who were allowed in as guests. Afterward, Robert met Maryann in the visiting room and he stayed for the day. So did her parents. Two weeks later, he arrived for a seventy-two-hour conjugal visit in the Family Living Unit, otherwise known as the FLU. This was the honeymoon. For two years, he came every week and there were conjugal visits every two or three months. But what did she know about him? A bride in prison finds it difficult to ask questions about her new husband's life. He was not like William, this new husband, but he'd done county jail time and he had a brother in prison. He was not unfamiliar with her life.

When his mother died, he came to the prison to tell her. He'd been drinking and doing cocaine. By coming to the prison in that condition, he might have put Maryann under suspicion of bringing drugs inside. So she told him off. "Don't forget, my mama just died!" Robert growled. "And don't forget you're my mama now."

"I told him I was nobody's mama, I was his wife, and if he couldn't get cleaned up, don't bother coming to visit."

So he didn't.

Two years later, he sent a money order. No word about where he'd been or what he'd been doing. Then he arrived— with a question: When could he have a FLU visit? Shortly after that, he vanished, along with her legal transcripts and a box of her things. Maryann laughed when I said her story wasn't funny. She said, "Next time, you do the talking." Her calls are limited to fifteen minutes. They are interrupted by a recorded voice telling us how much time we have left and reminding us that the call is being monitored, like every other minute of her life.

Topeka

33

That summer, Maryann's parole was denied for the eighth or ninth time. But this time was harder. This time hurt in a different way. Usually, the board said she showed no signs of remorse, or that she had no insight. They said she still had time to serve on her Hawaii sentence. They asked why she didn't just leave William, just walk out the door. But this time, she was denied parole when one of the commissioners said he didn't think there was enough time on Earth to forgive her. Forgive: to pardon, to overlook, to remit a debt or offense. To be merciful.

She wrote, "So that's it for now. Even though I knew I wouldn't be going anywhere just yet, there was still a small part of me that would have liked to have been found suitable just cuz. Cuz I am even though no suitability finding means anything right now. The governor isn't letting anyone out, even if we're approved. And he has the final say. Then the fact that

I've been going to these hearings for almost 25 years really hit me later that day. When will it end? And what if I don't win this writ in Hawaii . . . Everything just kind of came crashing in on me after the hearing. But I'm working on pulling myself out of it. I have to! I can't let these people get the better of me now!"

I have the transcript from one of her old hearings. It's from July 1992, and the presiding commissioner was Maureen O'Connell, who had presided at William's confessional hearing the year before. Maryann was represented by Deborah Fraser, who had been appointed by the state. Someone from the DA's office was present to represent the state of California, and there were two other commissioners and a correctional officer in the room. The hearing took place at the prison.

O'Connell starts with what she calls Maryann's "social history." "You are adopted. Your parents are in Arizona. Your adoptive parents are in Arizona. There's no prior criminal history. You graduated from high school. You got a job in your dad's firm. You met the crime partner, William Acker, got married to him, and then went on a three-week crime spree. There was a string of armed robberies here in California and then the murder. The incident in Hawaii occurred first. You never tried to get away from him?"

MARYANN: Yes, I did try to get away. I left while he was sleeping and I got about two blocks away.

O'CONNELL: So did he beat you after he found you gone?

MARYANN: He just held the gun to me and threatened to kill me if I tried again.

O'CONNELL: Well, you know, I don't hold your ex-husband in much regard because he is one of God's lowliest creatures,

but it is unfortunate . . . it's very
strange to me. If I was held captive
or felt I was a prisoner, I would do
anything in my power to get away. You
became involved with this guy who was
a parolee. You knew that. Two years
ago we talked about your parents and
why you did all this.

MARYANN: I've thought about it a lot since the
last hearing and in the last fourteen
years. I've thought about the whole
thing a lot and I didn't enjoy being
involved in the crimes and I didn't
enjoy the intimidation and fear that I
felt with him. And I've thought over
and over again of trying to figure out
maybe there was something different I
could have done and I'm still thinking
about that and I wish there had been
something or I had been thinking more
clearly at the time.

O'CONNELL: Well, you know, I'll state it again
for the record. I don't think you shot
either person. But I think you're
still equally as culpable as he is in
terms of needing to be punished and
taking the lumps for all of the
mistakes you made in judgment. My
feelings about him are, he snitched
everybody off in the State of
California and God knows where else,
and he left you hanging, holding
the bag in Hawaii. But you had an
opportunity to fix that and you didn't.
And so for the momentary lapse in

judgment you are suffering greatly
and the ones I feel sorry for are your
parents, not your real parents, but
your adoptive parents. Those are the
ones I feel the most sorry for in this
whole mess and of course the victim's
family. That's just a total waste, the
whole thing. Because clearly you had
the correct upbringing, you were
taught moral values. You were a
churchgoing person. Even if you
disagreed with the strictness of the
Mormon religion, and your dad and all
of that. I heard someone else tell me
that not too long ago, and I said you
mean to tell me you committed your
crime because your father believed in
God? Have you told them you're sorry?

MARYANN: Yes, I have. And they have asked me
where they went wrong and I have told
them over and over they didn't go
wrong anywhere. And I am sorry for
what I've put them through and I know
they've suffered a lot.

O'CONNELL: More than you'll probably ever know.

MARYANN: Probably.

At this point, the discussion moves on to Maryann's report card from the prison. She's been discipline-free. She's participated in psychotherapy groups and attended AA and NA groups. She is secretary to the Mexican American Association and has received a two-year college degree.

A second commissioner discusses Maryann's psychiatric report, which states that she has normal posture and gait, normal clothing, personal hygiene, mild to moderate defensiveness, and lack of insight. The second commissioner says, "What do you think Dr. Francis meant by that?"

MARYANN: I'm not sure. I probably do tend to get defensive at times . . .

COMMISSIONER: In terms of your being defensive . . . blaming . . . it appeared to me that your crime partner had a lot to do with the particular crime spree. And you could have left. You could have left in Hawaii and so forth. And you came across kind of like that. But that's my opinion. That's how I saw it. It seemed like it was William Acker's show and you were there for the ride, but you were kind of scared and so forth. I saw it that way. You don't have to agree with that, but that's how I saw it in terms of how the psychiatrist indicated.

MARYANN: I guess. I'm not saying that I don't accept responsibility. I know I am responsible to a degree for my actions.

COMMISSIONER: You say to a degree. How much to a degree? The conclusion on that report is compulsive personality disorder with passive-aggressiveness and dependent features. It says you appear to be tightly emotionally bound to your parent-child relationship even at the age of thirty-two. It says you are not

```
                        individuated from your parents.
                        What did Dr. Francis mean by that?
        MARYANN:    I'm not real sure other than my
                        parents are very important to me.
    COMMISSIONER:    Maybe you're not an independent
                        thinker. It says here the thrust of
                        psychological development would be
                        to begin addressing your feelings,
                        your self-identity, and your
                        relationship to other people. Dr.
                        Francis says her efforts to get you
                        to go in that direction were
                        analogous to trying to get you to
                        telephone Mars.
```

The third commissioner discusses various parole plans Maryann has submitted. There is an invitation from her biological father and his wife. There are job offers. The third commissioner says, "Do you know what's happened to your crime partner?"

```
        MARYANN:    No I don't. He's in the witness
                        protection program. They're floating
                        him around the United States.
```

The person from the DA's office makes a statement. She says that all of the crimes appear to have been carried out in a cruel, unfeeling, and calculated manner. She says a perfect example of that was the way the inmate and her crime partner used the last victim's car in the commission of other crimes. She says there was nothing in the file to indicate that Maryann was trying to escape when the police picked her up in Cesario Arauza's car and that, in fact, Maryann appeared to show no remorse at the time of her arrest. "So it is the people's position that she is still a threat to the public safety if she's granted release at this time."

Finally and in conclusion, Maryann's representative, Deborah Fraser, makes a speech. She'd read the article "Where Is William Acker?" in *California Legal Magazine* and told Maryann's family that it might be the means to get her paroled. Now she says:

> The district attorney has looked at
> this case for twenty-four hours.
> I've been with it for two years
> since I was first appointed. I've
> had an opportunity to take a close
> look at the crime partner, William
> Acker. I can understand where all
> of us sort of think that Maryann
> doesn't articulate real well and
> it's what to us appears to show a
> lack of remorse but is actually
> sort of an aspect of her
> personality which is not like mine.
> She is not Italian and she doesn't
> have that sort of effervescence.
> But that's Maryann. William Acker
> is a notorious squeal. He has
> testified in over thirteen capital
> cases and he's responsible for
> sending a man to death row. What's
> more, during Maryann's trial in
> California, her attorney was an ex-
> district attorney and Maryann was
> his first and last client. At the
> end of the trial he went back to
> the DA's office. He didn't even show

up for her sentencing. He waived
jury in a murder case. That's
absurd! And at the time that this
trial was going on, the judge was
under investigation for making
obscene phone calls. . . . This
case is real strange. And it's just
on and on as weird as it can be.
William Acker had told L.A.
Detective Ahn about the Hawaii case
and said he was doing it so his
wife could get psychiatric help.
Well, everybody sort of knows when
they deal with William Acker that
the one person who needs serious
psychiatric help is William Acker.
He's been in and out of jail since
he was six years old. Maryann
didn't know that at eighteen. I
think we all agree, except perhaps
for the district attorney, that
Maryann didn't kill anybody. She
never murdered a soul and yet she's
sitting here for two counts of
murder. Now she's got to be
responsible for those robberies and
at eighteen years old sometimes you
don't know your head from a hole in
the ground and you don't see a way
out. Acker is very good at what he
does. I had two cases I dug up
where he accused his ex-wife in
parcel with another robbery. They
dismissed against her. He got a
hundred and twenty days. And then

six months later he got out, after
six months he had another
girlfriend try to steal a car in a
parking lot in Zody. He tells the
cops she did it. She wasn't even
near the car. And he ends up doing
time and she ends up getting
probation. So this guy has got a
whole story behind him of accusing
other people of doing crimes in
which the crime partners have
little or nothing to do with it.
And this case is no different. What
he's done is he's accused his wife
of committing two murders and it is
on his testimony in Hawaii. How he
cut this deal, I don't know. But
she ends up going down with a 187
in Hawaii and he walks away with a
robbery. He did enough tactical
maneuvers in 1979 at that
California trial to avoid ever
having to stand trial with Maryann.
If he had had to stand trial with
her, I don't think she would be
here. I think that when the DA
talks about no remorse . . . you
couldn't describe William Acker
better. The man will do anything
and sell anybody to save
his own soul. In 1991 you were the
commissioner on his case when he
testified at his own parole hearing.
What's he say? Maryann didn't kill
anybody. And he finally . . .

O'CONNELL: Yes. I asked him the question
               specifically and I don't think I was
               as vehement toward him. I didn't
               tell him that he was the scum of
               the earth at that time, but he
               really is.

MS. FRASER: He really is. Is Maryann suitable
               for parole? You bet she is. She
               didn't murder anybody. She's spent
               fourteen years in this prison doing
               time and it hasn't been wasted.
               She's raised herself up from being
               a stupid kid at eighteen to being
               at least a decent smart kid at
               thirty-two. And I think it's time
               to let her go. She should be
               paroled. And William Acker ought to
               burn in hell for putting her here.
               She does take responsibility for
               her crimes, but what does she get?
               She didn't murder anybody and
               that's what she's doing time for.
               So if you want to talk about a
               reasonable risk, if you had to
               make a pitch to the governor, this
               is the one. This is the one.
               Maryann Acker is suitable and she
               should be out.

After this hearing, Maureen O'Connell voted to parole
Maryann. She is the only commissioner who ever has. Worse,
soon after the hearing, Deborah Fraser disappeared. Maryann
could not find her. When USC accepted Maryann's case in
1995, they could not find her. They needed the files and transcripts from previous hearings. Where was Deborah Fraser?

Dear Linda,

You want to know something that I am really looking forward to doing when I get out? I want to go grocery shopping. I want to get in a car and go to a store and buy some food and then cook it. And then something else. Going into a bathroom, shutting the door behind me, and taking a shower by myself and barefooted! The shower room, which is at the top of the hall, has three shower stalls and a bathtub. The partitions don't go all the way to the floor, so you get your feet splashed by the water from the other showers. Unless, on a rare occasion there's no one else in there, you can't just get a quiet, peaceful, relaxing shower. And, with 120 people sharing 8 showers (there is a shower room in each hallway), you don't dare go without shower shoes. And unless you thoroughly scour it before hand, you don't dare take a bath.

I just finished reading The House of Mirth and it struck me how the woman, Lily Bart, made a "career" out of climbing the social ladder and attempting to find an appropriate husband, all of which led to her demise. Women have come so far in some ways.

Love ya,
Maryann

34

August 2001. Maryann writes to tell me that she is making piñatas for the prison's Mexican American Association. The piñatas will be sent to schools and hospitals. There is a banquet planned for September 11. "Something fun to look forward to."

Then, when the World Trade Center is hit, there is an immediate call. I had thought of her as locked away monastically—as separate from news of the outside world as she was from its pleasures. But she listens to the radio at five o'clock every morning and she knew about the attacks before I did. A few minutes after her phone call, the prison yard was closed and the women spent the rest of that day locked down, as if the falling towers had made them suddenly dangerous. While they were on lockdown, more than six thousand dollars was collected among them. "In here it had a unifying effect," Maryann told me, adding that it's their country, too. "Our families are out there, remember, and our neighbors, and everything we care about."

It made me want to see my mother.

By late September, airport security had changed—everything had changed—and entering my birth country was a foreign experience. I had become an alien. It takes about seven hours, all told, to get from my front door in Toronto to my mother's Topeka house. I'd fly down, rent a car in Kansas City, and drive for an hour and a half. I'd ring the doorbell. Then, following the greeting, there was supposed to be the sniffing of rooms, the essential iced tea, although all of that had ended a few weeks before when I'd come home for the high school reunion. Like the country around her, my mother had ceased to be recognizable.

At the reunion, I'd learned that several of my old classmates were having similar problems with their parents. I hadn't seen these people for forty years, but they had taken my troubles to heart. I was given business cards, hugs, follow-up visits in the front yard, and the name of that place where the mother with Alzheimer's lived. "It's just what you need," the junior high crush had assured me. He of the white mustache. I had told him I'd suffered agonies in my great desire for him. We had danced. He was one of the boys with whom I had learned our unique local step. About my desire, he had kindly said, "I wish I'd known."

The other old flame—the one who ran off to the South Pacific—offered his legal services. Dennis was the first boy I kissed after my life-changing journey to Hawaii in 1958. I kissed him in the front yard, under the empty flagpole, although I realized that my new attractiveness was flavored by my desire for escape. Yes, coming back from so far away had given me a little mystery, and I clung to it.

The place my reunion dance partner mentioned was nice. I

had gone to look at it. There was a second-floor apartment available with balcony doors that looked straight into the branches of an oak, my mother's favorite tree. But how would I ever talk her into it? According to the county social worker, my mother couldn't, or didn't, feed herself, wash herself, remember dates, or show any interest in life. But she was legally in charge of herself. To go in another direction, to make myself her guardian, would be an indignity I couldn't bear to press on her.

Now, in her dark bedroom, a bundle of blankets was unresponsive. "Linda's here," said Sandee, who was employed by the county to be there every afternoon. The smell of uneaten chicken soup filtered in from the kitchen.

Mother rolled over and smiled, then rolled into her fetal position again.

"We're going to the hospital," I said nervously.

Mother said, "Not today. I don't feel well enough."

I cursed my brother for his plane crash. I wrung my hands and bit my lips and went to the living room and paced. Then I told Mother to get in my rented car or I would call an ambulance.

She locked herself in the bathroom but then came out twenty minutes later lipsticked and powdered and rouged. "My clothes . . ."

"You'll go in your robe." Sandee and I led Mother outside, all the way to the curb where I had parked my car. She seemed to be treading very carefully, as if there were hundreds of eggs on the grass. Or land mines. From the height of the curb, the passenger seat seemed to be miles away. We lowered her into it.

I didn't think that she was never coming back. I didn't think that she would be assigned to the locked mental ward of the hospital. I thought I was doing my best, and maybe I was. Her room in the mental ward had a mirror, a dressing table, a closet, a private toilet and washbasin. I kept thinking of prison, but Mother thought she was in a hotel.

Maryann called, but what news could she have that was

equal to this? "If it would help at all to talk," she said. She said how much she regretted not having been there with her parents when they were sick, when they needed her.

"I'm trying," I said. "But I live in another country." I was thinking of the months Mother had spent with me in Hawaii—a middle-aged widow and a young divorcée trying to be a family for two little girls. I wanted to tell Maryann how much I was missing my mother, but how could I explain the force she had been in my life?

I thought about mentioning my brother's death, saying that my mother was suffering a delayed reaction. But then I remembered Larry Hasker. I thought about Cesario Arauza. Ripples and ripples of grief.

"What does she care about most of all?" Maryann asked.

"Her pride and joy is her cat, Miss Pym," I said, "but when I'm at the hospital, she never mentions her."

Then Maryann told me about Nermal. Was this another attempt to cheer me? She said she'd been working for Inmate Day Labor, the prison construction crew where she was a clerk, keeping records of materials and orders for her boss, while the other women prisoners did electrical or plumbing or building work. This is her favorite job, but it's not dependable, because state projects often run out of money. The central unit needs a new roof, but that will have to wait. A housing unit needs to be rewired, but there is nothing in the budget for it. Still, prisoners have to work. They need money for tampons and shampoo and soap. They need money for food from the canteen and for pajamas and underwear. Stamps. Stationery. Besides, it's the law. Each of them has a five-day workweek, with the average pay being thirty-five cents an hour, although they never see any money; they have accounts that they draw against, the way coal miners used to draw against supplies at the company store.

It was while working for Inmate Day Labor that Maryann met the little cat named Nermal—"because he's not quite normal"—one of the many feral cats who lived on the prison grounds. Nermal had started watching Maryann during work hours, when the rest of the crew was outside. "I'd feed her lunch meat out of my box lunch because generally I won't touch the stuff anyway." Naturally, the little cat followed Maryann to the next job site. Every morning, she'd wait for her generous human friend at the gate she had to go through to get to work. When IDL completed the project and relocated, someone told Maryann that the cat was still waiting.

One day, Maryann was sent back to the old site to pick up some tools. She called and the little cat came running. Maryann took her to the new site, and she and Valere started showing her the way to their housing unit, until eventually Nermal took up residence on the meager windowsill of their cell. She said, "Now, about Miss Pym," and I tried to imagine Maryann's face, although I had no idea where she was sitting or standing. I couldn't imagine what it looked like where she lived. "Once I dreamed that I was getting ready to parole," she said. "I was trying to put Nermal into a box to take him with me, but before I could get the lid on the box, he jumped out and wouldn't come back. Linda, I was devastated."

I was following the story. It was a little diversion, nothing more, and our minutes were ticking away. Then she said that when the prison decided to cull the cats, she got frightened. There had always been rules. No pets for prisoners. No taming. No feeding. But now the ones they could find were going to be killed, and for the first time in days, I focused on something besides my mother or myself. When she said she had wangled permission to get Nermal out, I listened. She had arranged for permission to give her cat to Sheron, the faithful visitor. It was a sacrifice. To guarantee his safety. She took a long breath.

35

At the hospital, a woman named Velma invited me to sit down at the bingo table where she and my mother were sitting. My mother, never a player of games, sat there listlessly, while Velma was bouncy, imparting real urgency to the game. She took an interest in Mother, tracing her background and mentioning a friend they had in common. "Why, Jill Seegram! She's from my town."

At the mention of Jill Seegram, Mother's face brightened a shade.

"Why, I remember their place," Velma insisted. "That apartment over the store. They had some real good antiques."

"Jill always looked so refined," I added next. "With that ash-blond chignon. And her tweeds." There had been rumors about Jill and my father.

"Exactly!" Velma exclaimed. "But she's dead now," she

added respectfully, gazing at Mother. "You sure couldn't be her age."

Both of these assertions threw Mother back into confusion. These days she was frank about her age, although it had taken ninety years to make her so. Finally, she realized she could use it as an excuse. "I'm an old lady, for heaven's sake. It's fine if I want to stay in bed." When Mother told Velma her age, Velma said, "I don't believe it! Isn't she something?"

I remembered being driven down to the Seegrams' apartment one rare Sunday afternoon when my father didn't go back to the office. The apartment was huge, full of furniture that looked impressive in the dusty light. But something was wrong in that place. An old man and a beautiful wife. "You went to England with Jill after Dad died," I reminded my mother.

Now she looked at me. Really looked. "Yes, I did," she agreed. "She smoked all the time. Yes, that's right."

There were only certain hours I was allowed to visit my mother, so I spent the rest of my time going through her house, as if my attention to her basement, her desk, her closets would bring her back to herself. I made piles: to throw away, to give away, to clean—big bigger biggest. The closets were a heap of various vintages, thousands of shoes, mouse droppings, dead mice. At 2:20, I'd dash to the car and drive to the hospital, where I'd find Mother with Velma, although Velma's husband was often sitting nearby. All the ladies in the mental ward eyed him hungrily. "I'd like one of those," my mother whispered to me. Later it was simply, "I want him."

I told Mother that Miss Pym had been hiding in the closet, and she looked at me blankly. "I don't know what kind of hotel this is," she whispered. "Last night a big black girl just came right into my room." This with a snort of disbelief.

"It's a hospital," I would say during conversations like this.

"Why would I be in a hospital? There's nothing wrong with me."

"Remember how tired you've been? You've been flat in bed for six weeks."

"That's a lie."

In our family, there was a current of popular language that never saw the light of day. Mother would say, "Linda Jane, don't fib." Her strongest words of censure were "That's vulgar," the lowest jibe. So this was a new departure, a new, uncensored mother. "Anyway, I'm going home tomorrow. They're not doing anything for me here."

"But I saw your schedule on the board. You had exercise this morning and a group meeting. You worked with leather."

"I hated that. Imagine, with all the things I've done in my life, and I couldn't lace that silly shoe."

Velma had been standing in the doorway. Now she entered the room and patted Mother's knee. "Leather's hard," she acknowledged. "It's a whole different skill from other things."

Mother was right about the things she'd done in her life. In the closet, I found I. Miller shoes, delicious fruited hats, and beautiful sweaters, many of them knit, purled, lined, and decorated by my mother. I could remember occasions for each of her outfits—skirt, blouse, jumper, coat—all made by a dressmaker, to be arranged and rearranged. As a girl, evaluating the many possibilities, as with paper dolls, I was entranced. No store-bought clothes came near the imaginative variations or style of my mother's wardrobe. A pair of alligator pumps on platform soles, a matching purse—these were treasures that could not be traded, sold, given, or trashed. But I went on filling clear plastic bags, because over the past several years, whether because of failing eyesight, failing nerves, or despair, Mother's excellent housekeeping skills had disappeared. The evidence of neglect was there in the closet, where several small creatures had died,

no doubt miserably, and where I found small bones and cob-
webs and unsorted papers and every canceled check ever signed
by my father, going back to the 1930s. Once I had filled the
plastic bags, I washed the shelves and began to reconstruct the
closet as it might have been. My favorite dresses were hung on
hangers my grandmother had covered with crochet work. Several pairs of shoes in their original boxes were put back on the
upper shelf. Bags were arranged, even ornaments. It was a
memorial to my mother made of her own artifacts.

She kept an old footstool in that closet—a wooden box
with an upholstered lid and a slipcover. Over the years, she had
used it to hide her silverware and her jewelry. "Who would
bother to look in it?" she'd always say, and now opening it felt
like a case of bad manners, as if she might suddenly jump in her
Oldsmobile and drive home, sweep through the door carrying
groceries, the dry cleaning, the mail, and find me in flagrante.

"Oh my God! Sandee! Come in here!"

Sandee was cleaning the kitchen shelves. She waded
through the dining room, into the bedroom, past the bureau,
and over to me. "A .357 Magnum," she intoned with a big
intake of breath. "Beautiful!"

The last of my father's guns.

"You could take it to the cops."

"No way."

Dying with his boots on, collapsing of a heart attack during
a courtroom argument (defending a client he distrusted and
disliked), my father had left a legacy of thirteen loaded guns.
Spell spaghetti. *Seventeen times thirty-eight. Now!* Holding his
gun put my father's voice into my head and my hand began to
shake. "I'm sure it's not registered. Anyway, they'd sell it."
Raised to be more suspicious of cops than of robbers, I tucked
the gun back into its sheepskin holster and told Sandee about
the day my brother had taken us—what was left of the
family—out to Mission Creek, which ran through a piece of
land my father had bought when he was already out of money

or time to build on it. My father had planned to erect an adobe house there, brick by handmade brick. Skip told Mother to choose one of the thirteen guns and, while children and grandchildren watched, she chose her weapon, loaded it, and took aim at a log that was bobbing along in the muddy water of the creek. I have a photograph of this moment—Esta's wide eyes and my brother with his shirt off, looking straight ahead, as if we were proving ourselves against a common enemy, although the only one we shared was Death.

"You never tell me anything," I'd heard Velma say to Mother. And I might have said the same. There were the rumors about Jill Seegram and all the others, even the mother of that boy in my class, my father's ward. I used to imagine that he was a brother, and maybe he was. Maybe he was a secret my father and I kept, like the clients he visited when I was in the car with him, broken women, chain-smoking. "Your father was crazy about you" is what Mother used to tell me, as if any failure of affection between us was mine. She never complained about his temper and seemed not to notice that he terrified and humiliated me, that I was expected, at all hours, to be without blemish, to perform on demand. *Spell* pragmatic. *Now! Sound it out.* In his presence, I'd make myself small, being careful not to give him reason to notice me. *Do you want to come inside for your spanking or take it out here in front of your friends?* Hearing his car in the driveway when he came home for dinner, I'd go to my bathroom and lock the door. Sometimes I'd be sick. "I have nothing to tell" is what Mother would say to Velma. "I'm a happy person, except for being here." But while she was there, propped up in her hospital bed, I suddenly wanted to shout at her. Lies! Lies lies lies! I wanted to shake this mother who had kept herself blind and silent. I wanted to rail at this old woman who was too far gone to defend herself. What had come over me? All my life, I had wanted only to make her happy, but her happiness depended on something entirely false. She had ignored my father's behavior toward me, but that wasn't all.

After Philip ran away to Mexico, she made me promise to stop seeing another boy. I was hurting her reputation. "What you do in Boulder gets back to Topeka, don't forget." She and my father had driven across the whole state of Kansas and into the mountains of Colorado to deliver this ultimatum. It was then that I made my call to Mexico. It was after that afternoon that I ran away with Philip.

"We have your mother on a new medication," one of the nurses announced later that day when I visited her in the hospital. "These things work their wonders fast in the elderly."

The next day, I rented the apartment that looked right into the branches of the tall oak tree. The wonder of people, like stories, is that they are mutable, or so I like to think. When ten days had passed and I walked Mother out of the locked ward and into the elevator, she had gone down the darkest hole of her life and come out the other side. She said she was ready to go home, and I said, "We're going to your new apartment. With a nice tree and birds."

"I need to go home first and get my clothes. And what about Miss Pym?"

I told her the cat, her clothes, her books, and her furniture were waiting at the new address, and we drove there without incident, without passing Go or collecting two hundred dollars or bursting into tears. Mother looked out the passenger side of the car at the town she had adopted seventy years before. She watched it go by. And at her new door, one she had never entered before, she invited me in for iced tea.

36

That gun of my father's was a beautiful object perhaps, but it was something I wanted not to exist, as I want all guns not to exist. Anyway, I would never be able to take it back with me to Canada, where handguns are prohibited, just as they should be.

As if my father's spirit were embedded in the gun, I could feel its weight all that week, while Mother was settling into the apartment and I slept in her more or less empty house. Knowing the gun was there, in the closet, full of my father, I did not feel safe. Knowing the decision of what to do with it was mine to make, and that my father was somehow involved, I actually could not sleep. There must be a right answer, I told myself. Where my father was concerned, there was always a right answer. And my problem, eternal, was to find it.

Word problems, tests. I began to wonder what had happened to the other guns—twelve—which he had left in various places when he died—under the front seat of his Lincoln, in the basement, in his desk. . . . I wondered why he had wanted so many guns—a man who believed they were useful for one purpose only. "Never pick up a gun unless you intend to use it. Never shoot unless you intend to kill."

Like that man on the jury, Mr. Sugai.

My father kept a gun in his handkerchief drawer.

"Is it loaded, Daddy?"

"Of course it is."

I used to put his handkerchiefs away after they were ironed. I used to touch the strange skin of this gun. I used to watch my father get dressed in the morning, putting on his undershirt first and then his socks. Boxers, starched shirt, suit pants, tie— always in the same order. Finally the jacket. And nakedness always part of our family life. I watched him open and shut the drawer, unfold a handkerchief, tuck it and his wallet into the right back pocket.

It didn't occur to me until years later that only when one of us was naked did I feel safe. At those moments, we were like dogs with our bellies exposed. Paws up. You don't ask a naked girl to do arithmetic. Peeling the vegetables, cleaning the sink, sweeping, or vacuuming, I was bound to irritate.

It was while vacuuming that I finally rebelled. There had been a dinner party the night before and I was put to cleaning the Oriental rug before we went out someplace. A long drive, I think, it was going to be.

The table had been shoved off the rug. It sat, large and polished, in its unusual situation, relegated to the margins of the room. I had followed orders. Had pulled the vacuum quietly in from the broom cupboard near the back door. I was wearing a full skirt, already dressed for our departure. Dressed up, because that was the way things were in those days. One of my duties was to be pretty, smile, stand up straight, walk with my shoulders back, toes forward. Once, I had mentioned to my father that ballerinas walk with their toes angled out, but my father said, "Nonsense," and kept his eyes on my feet.

I was prepared for constant scrutiny; it was a fact of life. Maybe, on some level, I was even prepared for the rage that boiled up in my father when he saw me plug the old Hoover in and start across the rug with it. Anyway, I should have known it was coming. I was doing something he had told me to do, but I was doing it wrong, as always and as usual. Still, I pushed the vacuum. Back and forth, back and forth. I pushed and pulled until my father grabbed the handle and yanked it away. "This instant. Right this minute! Do it correctly!" Beside himself, if that phrase means what I think it means. But when I tried again, pushing and pulling, every swipe was worse, more terrible, more a blow to what he knew vacuuming ought to be. He stood there shouting and grabbing, but I could not get it right. I was too fast, too slow. I was pushing randomly. I wasn't pulling back all the way. My crying always made things worse, so I tried to control my breath, but the tears were starting. No show of emotion! He wouldn't stand for it. "I'll give you something to cry about." He grabbed and shouted and squeezed until I sank to my knees, skirt billowing out, face on the rug— colors I knew from rolling around down there with our dog.

It was the only protest I had ever made, but it ended something.

I refused to get up.

My mother fled upstairs and sat in a chair in the guest room, where she never sat. She was crying. "I don't like you. Either of you."

Now, as I tried to sleep alone in my mother's house with my father's gun, so many images came back from the past that I'd get up and drink a glass of milk and begin to attack her library. Because, if my father had guns, my mother had books. There were mysteries, art books, cookbooks, novels, and histories. The political lives of FDR, Truman, and Adlai Stevenson—her heroes. Anthropology, biblical scholarship, decorative design, and ballet. I tried to sort them and then gave up. I told people to drop by and take some home. I called the library.

I solved the gun problem privately. All by myself, I took an evening drive. It felt appropriate, once I had thought of it, because my father had had a sailboat, which was the love of his life. The truth is that most of the time, year after year, it was in dry dock in our garage. My boyfriend helped sand it. My brother helped sand it. My father worked on it at odd hours of the night to ease the pain in his back from a war injury. The boat was wood, a Thistle, designed in Scotland. And it was decidedly the fastest, definitely the loveliest boat on Lake Shawnee. But when my father got elected to the school board, there was no time for sanding, and the boat developed a serious case of dry rot, which meant it was never where it was designed to be. For years, we stored yard equipment and grass seed in its shapely hull, and it became a not very funny family joke. Still, I remember a few hours of early childhood when riding the surface of the lake brought me close to bliss. My father had made me a seat up in the bow and we often sailed at night, when I could feel the swell of wind from the billowing jib and count the comforting rhythm of the flashing red-and-green warning light. Up there, riding the dark surface of the lake, I was under his protection but happily out of reach. My father directed his temper at the sails and lines. He yelled like a captain at my mother, but he more or less forgot about me.

It was, therefore, a sort of tribute, a kind of memorial to my father, when I heaved the last of his guns—the beautiful .357 Magnum—into the water near a place where the boat had been moored in the years before I started fourth grade. I watched it sink. I could not throw the gun very far and the water was not very deep. Wondering whether some bad person might see it or find it or fish it up and put it to evil use, I hovered at the shoreline. I felt slightly silly. I felt apologetic. It seemed to me that I should apologize to my father. It seemed to me that I should indulge in an appropriate rite. Eventually, though, I turned on my heels and went back to my rented car. There is very little to be said about such events. As I drove away, traveling the bumpy road we had driven so many times, so many years ago, I had to admit to myself that throwing the gun in the lake was not a tribute to my father, but exactly the opposite. I had buried his gun in the waters of Lake Shawnee out of spite.

37

Maryann's father was born a Baptist, like mine, but when Maryann talks about him, I notice the pride and affection in her voice and feel jealous of their relationship. He came into his manhood during the Depression, like my father. While my father was selling silk stockings door-to-door, Bert Bray was selling tires in East Texas. He was also paid to collect on bills when drought, dust storms, and wind took out three wheat crops in a row. He'd hoped to be a pharmacist, but when he was still a boy, his father died and he went to work for the family. That was his character. Loyal. Warm. Near the end of his life, he typed out a letter on fifteen single-spaced pages for his surviving children and for his three grandchildren, for whom he must still have felt some shred of hope. Penne found the letter after he died and eventually sent a copy to Maryann. The sentences run off the paper at the bottom, but Maryann says that was just like her father, who refused to waste anything, even space.

"Sometimes I would encounter a distraught and angry farmer," he wrote about the years he spent collecting on bills. "I have been run off with a shotgun, hay hook, and fence post. I would drive my truck into his yard, turn it around leave the engine running, both doors open and by this strategy could get away with a whole skin."

When things dried up completely, Bert decided to join the great exodus to California, but he stopped in Phoenix on the way. It was 1939, and he looked around at the town. It was a whole lot better than East Texas, and he found a job there pretty easily, riding the bus from Mesa into Phoenix every morning, taking the route that Doug, the first boyfriend, must have taken to visit Maryann's apartment in 1978. Mesa to Phoenix. The road of romance for Maryann and her mother. "There was a real cute girl who rode the bus from Mesa. I wanted to get acquainted with her but had a problem as she always sat with her girl friend and I had difficulty talking to her. I finally got a break. Her friend was ill one day and she saved me a seat by her. She denies she saved me the seat but I don't believe her."

When Gladys moved to Phoenix, she was "much more available for serious romance and I tried to sweep her off her feet. Didn't work out that way. She was a serious conservative lovely Mormon girl and made me use all my skill to convince her I was her knight in shining armor."

They went to movies. They went to dances. At the end of an evening out, they would pass her house and keep walking two more blocks to a coffee shop, where they could talk the rest of the night. "I decided if I was ever to get enough sleep to stay alive I had to change my tactics and see if the woman would marry me."

On December 7, 1940, they began married life in a small

apartment. A baby boy was born a month before Pearl Harbor and they named him Butch. He was to provide them with a bonding tragedy. As I read the letter written so many years later, I am alert to Bert's casual dismissal of disaster and his joking references. Although the baby's death, caused by that paper clip that pierced his throat, must have caused unfathomable heartbreak, Maryann's father does not betray his feelings. There was an infection. The child was six months old. Then there is this: "Gladys was and is a life long member of the Church of Jesus Christ of Latter Day Saints and believing that Butch would be returned to her to raise in the millennium helped her to overcome the terrible loss and face the future with hope. She convinced me this was true and it helped me too. We took up our lives and walked straight into WW2."

Bert and my father were both in the navy, stationed in the Philippines. It seems possible that they knew each other there. It's a coincidence that I cannot help imagining. I have a folded piece of paper on my desk—a memento of that time. It's the menu for Christmas dinner, 1944—a drawing of candles lighting up the word *Liberation*. "After Three Years" is written underneath the candles. And "In the Philippines." The dinner began with an orange basket and chilled tomato juice. There were olives, sweet mixed-pickle relish, pineapple and cheese salad, turkey supreme soup, and roasted tom turkey with sage dressing and giblet gravy. There were snowflake potatoes, cranberry sauce, buttered carrots, and peas. There were roasted sweet potatoes, whole-kernel corn, and Parker House rolls. Chocolate milk, demitasse, hard candy, and "home baked" pumpkin pie. To the left of the menu was a group of signatures my father had collected. A few are indecipherable, but right in the middle is the signature of Douglas MacArthur, a man my father despised, who had written underneath, "May God preserve and protect you all—is my Christmas prayer." I've searched among the names for Bert Bray's, and while I can't see it, I like to imagine him there.

At that time, I was barely alive and Maryann was a long way from being born. Gladys had given birth to a second son a few months after Bert shipped out. When he left Australia for New Guinea, he was located in a place where the Japanese had been entrenched. "I still remember their privy," he writes. "It was built of split bamboo with a floor of bamboo over the holes in the ground. The holes in the floor were cut square and the edges were neatly laced with bamboo and covered with bamboo mats. Between each hole, a two-foot-high curtain of woven grass was hung. I thought that was pretty neat compared to a slit trench the GIs sometimes used."

I have a tiny photograph of a man from New Guinea left among my father's papers. The man is bare-chested, with wild, starchy hair. There is a note on the back: "man of the admiralties." Maybe our fathers met out there in the aboriginal Pacific. And then, back in Manila in June 1945, they might have met all over again as they were being shipped out. In September, Bert's outfit was decommissioned and he went home via Hawaii, just as my father did. It was in Hawaii, jumping to the ground from his plane and then catching his heavy pack, that my father sustained his only apparent war injury. Two weeks in Pearl Harbor for the returning soldiers and Maryann still so far in the future that a small stitch in time might have changed everything. If she'd been born an hour later, a day later . . . if she'd been given to another family . . . if Gladys and Bert had divorced . . . if Bert had been killed . . . if the second son had not died . . . Maryann would never have met William. And perhaps Larry Hasker would still be alive and Cesario Arauza, as well. But Gladys met Bert in L.A., where they had a brief second honeymoon. They danced at the Paladium Ball Room, visited the beach, and wandered around hand in hand. It was exactly the kind of honeymoon Maryann would try to replay with William.

I wonder if Bert's new son met his father the way I met mine, by locking myself in the upstairs bathroom the day he came home from the war. "I found a strange thing had happened to me," Bert writes. "I couldn't make a decision. Having all my thinking done for me by the navy for three years had impeded the process of thinking things through and reaching a decision." Bert went back to work as a salesman for McKesson, working the streets of Phoenix. In his letter, he calls himself "an honest con man." "I have tried many times to explain my fascination with selling and the only explanation I could verbalize is it is great sport to get an intelligent man to spend his money for my products. It is a one on one contest usually played on his turf." Gladys was working three days a week and they managed to pay off the bills that had resulted from Butch's accident and death.

Penne was born in 1950, the same year William Acker was born in Illinois. Brother Mike, the second son, had developed asthma when he was two or three years old, but by the time he was twelve, he was playing shortstop on a baseball team that Bert coached. Consummate father, he had been active in the Mormon Church since his marriage to Gladys, but it was Mike's death, at the age of fourteen, that made him decide to be baptized. Gladys could finally have their marriage sealed in the temple. Bert would now be a lay priest and Gladys would have her ticket to the Celestial Kingdom.

The daughters to whom Bert writes his letter actually number three. He says:

I need to include a paragraph about two other members of our family I have not touched on. About two or three months after Mikes passing Gladys came home with a two month baby girl. This came about through a friend Mary Sorsenson. She was a court clerk and heard of this baby girl being put up for adoption and decided we needed a baby to replace our sons. She sure put our minds to thinking in a different direction and helped us over the hard spots. Penne was missing Mike a lot and found some solace in coping with a new baby sister. She like Mike before her thought we were replacing her in our affections with the baby. She came to know better and helped Gladys cope with the new child in our lives. The other member I mentioned was Polly, a Navajo girl we received in our home on the Indian placement program of the Church. We had her three years and learned to love her a great deal. We still hear from her once in a while. I want my daughters to know I am proud to be known as their father and I love them very much. I admire their spirit and the way they strive to cope with life and its blessings and problems. I am going to leave the telling of their life story to them and explain I realize I have wrote more about the boys than the girls not because I found their lives less interesting or compelling but they are still here to write of their own. I encourage them to keep a journal which will make writing their history much easier and more complete. I would doubly encourage my Grand Children start now and keep a journal all their lives. I want Brandy, Jess, and Shannon to know I love them and am proud of them. I would ask them always to remember they are Heavenly Fathers children and He wants them to develop the talents he has given them and live clean lives that they may return to his kingdom and dwell there with Him and their Grandparents and parents forever.

By the time Maryann read Bert's letter, she had been in prison for twenty-two years.

38

W hat happened to Polly?" I ask Maryann when she calls.
"I guess she lives on the Navajo reservation, but she
doesn't have a phone, so I'm not really sure. I'd love to find her.
She's the only one I have left, and we were really, really close."

"She spent how many years with you?"

"Five. Six. I don't know. She went home in the summer,
then came back every fall. Then one year, she just didn't come
back."

"You haven't seen her since?"

"A couple of visits at home. Once we stayed up all night
talking. We were always like that. Oh, I miss Pauline. She came
here for an hour with one of her kids a long time back. Maybe
nineteen or twenty years ago."

When Gladys and Bert took Polly as a foster child, they
gave her a bed in Maryann's room. For Polly, it must have been
strange. In the summer, she was told to follow her mother's

native religious practices, and in the winter she pretended devotion to Jesus. At first, Polly spoke no English, but by the end of her first year with the Brays, she had lost huge chunks of her Navajo language. The year that Maryann turned eleven, when Polly did not come back, Gladys made a trip up to the reservation and argued with Polly's parents, who seemed to resent her influence. Polly was becoming too white. And there was all that religious training. But Maryann was bereft. No more foster sister. Why? Then Penne married. Officially, black people are relegated, by the Mormon Church, to a special, separate, and lowly status because God has cursed them with dark skin. Unofficially, the Brays were shunned. Living in preparation for the Second Coming of Christ, one doesn't question the bishop, or the elders in the church, but when Maryann began to question those closer to hand, Bert and Gladys must have prayed for their doubting child. Suddenly, there was a side to her they couldn't reach. Why tell her about the wild mother who gave her away, if not as a warning?

Packing up, leaving Phoenix saddened and disgraced, the Brays moved to Yuma, where there was something—a meeting of the youth group, a stake dance or a ward dance, or a society meeting—every night of the week. But in Yuma, there were also kids who hung out at the river. "I started ditching school quite a bit. My parents tried to set limits for me, but I ignored them and did what I wanted, and when Mother gave me her Volkswagen, it got easier. Once, I was driving away from school on my way to the river and I passed my dad. I had to make up a story, but I was getting good at that."

Yuma was a town of 25,000 souls in the southwest corner of Arizona. The Mormon Church had divided it into stakes, as it divides every town and city into stakes. It had divided the stakes into wards, as it always does. Yuma, on the east bank of the Colorado River, near the confluence of the Gila, was deep in Mormon country, Mormon mentality. Regulation, regulation, discipline. Growing up in a family in which the notion of

Mormons as the chosen people permeated every minute of life, Maryann's hold on identity must have been tenuous. Shunned by the chosen people, her parents kept insisting that she had been sent to Earth to choose between right and wrong, that she had the earthly treasure of free will. But was she one of them? What about her birth mother? Maybe all her attempts to be worthy were fraudulent.

During high school, she got her first job, as a cashier, then a second job as a salesperson at the new JCPenney. When she got laid off there, she went to work at Kmart, and one night when she was coming home from work, she got rear-ended at a stoplight. Because of the whiplash injury she sustained, her parents' insurance agent wrote her a check, and she decided to take a vacation and visit an aunt and uncle in San Jose. "I actually contemplated moving up there. Probably should have. Instead, I went back."

What if . . . ?

I tell Maryann there are a hundred things I would rewrite in my life, almost from the beginning. And there are things I would give myself, including an ounce of her confidence in fate. "My first job was at JCPenney, too," I announced one night when she called. "Isn't that strange? There are so many similar things in our lives."

"Did you get laid off?"

"I did. I only lasted a week. And I never shopped there after that. I went to work in my father's office from then on, every vacation. He said we might as well keep the money in the family, which wasn't especially flattering."

"Did you want to be a lawyer?"

"I wanted to be an architect, like my brother. But I was a girl. My parents thought I should learn stenography in case I didn't get married or my husband died in some tragedy."

"I just wanted to be. Anything. Live my life. I had that wild streak from my birth mother, I guess."

"You know, psychologists say kids who feel abandoned

are excessively dependent. On friends, on boyfriends, on husbands."

Maryann has heard this before. "I'm past that."

"But that's why you listened to William." Sometimes I spent entire phone conversations doing this, looking for things that made sense of her life or offered some sense of connection between us—JCPenney, fathers, Yuma. "My great-grandfather went out there and tried to settle a land claim. The letters he wrote home make it sound like the end of the Earth." With each discovery, it was as if I had come upon some proof. We had both had cockapoos. We had both lost purses at Disneyland! And found them. "They told me that nobody steals there." "We have a unique bond," Maryann had said, that last afternoon in the prison visiting room, but I could tell that she was not really interested in the little links I forged. Again and again, I asked Maryann to tell me about the house where she lived in Phoenix, "growing up, when you were still happy. I know you don't want to go back, but I think something must have happened there that made William the next part of your life." I didn't say that the freedom of a girl who runs away at seventeen is not really freedom, not for a while, not while she is running away. A girl who is desired feels powerful, but a girl who leaves home at seventeen is bound to look for everything she's fled from: authority, control.

The weight of it.

In that girlish white suitcase!

And what she finds will challenge everything she was taught to believe.

I didn't tell Maryann that I was learning a lot about myself and my past while I learned about her. As far as Maryann was concerned, I was a nice woman from a foreign country who was taking an interest in her. It seemed to suffice, but then sufficiency is relative.

It was at Kmart, in her senior year of high school, that Maryann met Doug, the man she abandoned for William. "Six foot two, with sandy brown hair. But what attracted me was how gentle he was, taking pictures of kids." Doug went from store to store, town to town. He worked a Kmart and other places. He lived in a suburb of Phoenix and that settled it. Maryann told her parents she would not be going to Arizona Western, the junior college in Yuma, although they had offered to pay her tuition. Instead, at the age of seventeen, she drove off in a car that had been her mother's. "I was hell-bent on getting back to Phoenix."

Which was easy for me to understand. I remember kissing my high school boyfriend good-bye when I left for college. We promised each other all kinds of things, but I was hell-bent, too. Away From Home, that's where I wanted to be. I went away to school and fell in with a group of strangers. I was free of my mother. I was free of my father. I didn't know I would never go back.

And there she is out in her driveway on an evening when she is still seventeen. There is a warm breeze. She's sitting in the little Volkswagen. There is a six-pack in the trunk and a pack of cigarettes in her purse and the breeze is a song coming through the trees. She's turning on the radio, waving to her mother, who stands at the window, partly hidden by the fluffy curtain, looking sad and furtive. Good-bye!

Maryann was president of the Young Adult Group at church, where she took Doug to dances. "Were you in love?"

"Not enough."

"But you thought you were."

"Not enough. Not enough."

"But . . ."

"I thought we'd get married eventually."

Doug had spent two years in South America on his mission, but he was living with his parents again. When Maryann moved to Phoenix, they saw each other whenever he was in town. He was twenty-five. A nice man. Good to her. And they sinned. Premarital sex is compared by the Mormon Church to murder. In fact, Doug was excommunicated because he'd slept with Maryann. But while he was gone, taking pictures of other people's children, she went out with William. Then she took him home. She had an apartment, a job. Father, mother. Friends. She had Doug, too. But she wanted William.

39

I spent the summer of 2002 at our house on the river, sitting at the table where I'd first written to Maryann two years before and watching three new robin hatchlings squeeze against the edges of their nest. I had just come back from another visit to New York, where it had seemed important to stand at the brink of Ground Zero and stare into the massive hole where the Twin Towers had once stood. I wanted to grapple with it for myself and for Maryann, who could not visit the pit with its trucks and cranes. It was an ugly pit except for the sheets of weathered paper covered in plastic and hung on a surrounding chain-link fence. REMEMBER ME . . . name, age, photograph. The flowers and mementos were pretty well abused by a long winter and a great many tears. And there was no particular order to anything. A man in a hard hat spoke Polish to a group of listeners. A man sweeping a marble stairway told me that yes, I was in part of the original building . . . where there were still signs pointing to elevators and restaurants that no longer exist.

While I was away, Maryann had been trying to call. There were messages left in both English and Spanish. "You have a call from an inmate in a California state prison . . . *quien es una presa de una facilidad.* . . . If you do not want to receive this call, press seven. . . . If you never want to receive a call from this institution again, press six. . . . If you accept the charges for this call, press five. . . ." What she wanted was to tell me about seeing an old video of her parents.

The video had been made the year after Maryann's Hawaii trial. She was told about it by another prisoner, who worked for In Service Training, where they had been going through the old video files. This one had been made by a television station for a program about California prisons. Maryann and her parents were in a segment on the Family Visiting Program. "I had never seen it," she told me when we finally connected. "And I didn't see the whole thing, but of the people I saw in the video, there are only three of us still in this facility. There was one gal named Goldie, who had probably been here for a couple of years when this was done. They asked her how long she would be here and she said 1985, which is exactly what I thought, too, because at that time, we still believed we'd get out at our minimum eligible parole date." Maryann's voice sounded dry. No wonder. In 1983, she was sure she had only another two years in prison. "She's still here for killing a man who was molesting her infant daughter," Maryann whispered. "We're both still here."

The video was hard to watch. "I don't even know that I can put into words how it affected me. The first flash of Mom actually took me by surprise. I almost didn't recognize her. Her voice, when she began to speak, sounded so foreign. Was that because I only remember the last time I spoke with her before she died, when she was so sick? Dad was just Dad—his voice and mannerisms. Maybe I haven't really grieved my loss. Maybe I just put it away."

I thought about those pictures hanging around the Trade Center pit, and the pit itself, which was like one of the circles of hell. While I walked the circumference, I had been looking for a picture of Kristin's friend Heather Ho, although the last time I'd seen her, in Hawaii, she was a thirteen-year-old girl wearing braces and a baseball cap. Heather had worked all her life to be a baker and she had a prestigious job at Windows on the World, up at the top of Tower 1. But why was I thinking of her while Maryann told me about seeing the old video? Part of me hadn't wanted to find Heather Ho. Part of me had wanted to think she wasn't there among the other victims and weather-scarred photographs. In Mexico, there is a simple handmade cross to mark every highway death. Driving, you see the crosses at hairpin turns or steep drops. But there are other, unmarked spots on this Earth. The tarmac where my brother crashed his plane, the highway, on the cloverleaf outside L.A., where Cesario Arauza was shot, and a place high above the waves at Hanauma Bay, where Larry Hasker took his last breath.

I was standing by the table I use as a desk at the cottage. Looking through the window, I could see the fledglings and, behind them, unlimited green, although there was the dusty road winding up between trees. I said, "But you don't even mention your own young self, Maryann. Locked away for so much longer than you expected ... didn't you feel any pity looking at that twenty-three-year-old girl?"

She said she hated the way she looked. She had a shoulder-length perm.

I said, "None of us likes to look at our old perms ... but it's possible to feel some nostalgia for our innocence."

Maybe it was the wrong word to use. Maryann was quiet for a while. Then she said, "I find myself stuffing the emotions I feel."

"I know you do. The parole boards always say you show no remorse. No insight. Could you let go of that control?"

"I can't. Not in here."

"Because you might say something or get in trouble?" People listen. People report on one another.

"I guess I've learned to hold myself in check." Voice flat. "It's the way to survive in here."

"And what's going on with your lawyer?" Mike Brennan's project at the University of Southern California's law school is designed to help people who are wrongfully convicted. It was started in 1980 as a way to help men in federal prisons, but in 1993 the law students began reading letters from women at CIW. When they read Maryann's, it did not look promising. All they had to go on was William's 1991 parole-hearing confession, and in Hawaii the judge at the court of appeals did not think William's confession provided sufficient reason to reopen the case. Recanting is viewed as suspect. Instead, USC chose a habeas plea, based on William's unreliability as a witness.

"We thought the testimonies were all destroyed, but Mike's got hold of the old files from the prosecutor's office in Hawaii," Maryann announced. "Which is huge. Because in those files there was a letter no one had seen before, at least no one on my side of the case. It's from Willy Ahn, the old detective in L.A. He sent it to Jan Futa a month before the trial in 1982. And it details William's sentence. Life with the possibility of parole. It's stamped, dated the day it was received, signed by Jan Futa. Which proves they let Bill perjure himself. The prosecutors knew he was lying on the witness stand. It also proves they withheld evidence from the defense. That's criminal."

I was looking out at the road. It was empty. From the kitchen, there was the smell of chicken cooking on the stove. Garlic and soy sauce. Maryann was talking and I was remembering a dream. I'd been involved in two murders. Not committing them, but watching. Am I guilty? I wrestle with this, regretting my own paralysis—although it wasn't exactly that. It was an interested passivity. I had stood aside, aware of enormous space all around me.

40

One night in August, the voice was flat again. Something was wrong, but it took a while to get there, and then, because of the minutes ticking on our call, she had to do it fast. "She needed a small bit of surgery," Maryann told me, speaking about a woman she didn't name. "Went in last week. I think it was a prolapsed uterus thing, or bladder. Nothing much. And she came back three days ago. We've been friends for a long time. She was here when I came in. But yesterday morning when she got out of bed, she complained of chest pains. That was it. She'd been given a release date in 1983, but they kept putting it off. They gave her seven to life, like the California judge gave me—not a death sentence, but that's what it was. And she was a person who was always good to everyone in here. There's such a cloud over us now—inmates and staff—everyone loved her. And she died in here."

"I'm so sorry."

"And today *Dateline* came in to do some interviews. What a time for it. We told them what happened. Then they interviewed a woman with leukemia. She had one leg amputated already and now she's had another one off. She should be gone. She's been here twenty years."

When the call came, I had just peeled my first ear of corn. All through August, we enjoy corn on the cob soaked in ice water and then grilled in its husks. We'd been in the river and we were drinking a bottle of cold wine. The house was hot, but there was a little breeze coming in through the screens and the sounds of the river and birds getting settled for the night. When I answered the phone, I mentioned the corn. Then I bit my lip.

Sherrie Chapman, the inmate with cancer, had died a few months before, after being denied a compassionate release. And death must be impersonal in prison, where someone simply disappears in the night, where there is no funeral, no official mourning, no way to signal grief. Maryann said everyone was suffering mentally and physically. Daytime temperatures were over one hundred degrees and the brick buildings held the heat long after the sun set for the night. At 8:30 p.m., the women were locked in hot cells with their six-inch electric fans. But there was one short reprieve. At 8:40, six rows of electronic buttons began to open the cell doors in rotation so the prisoners could sign up for phone calls. At 9:00, they were locked in again—no more chance to catch a little breeze, phone conversations finished. Maryann relished our conversations as a few minutes of relief.

For me, they were something else. The two people I spoke to most often on the phone that summer were an old woman and a prisoner, neither of whom I could save. When I wasn't talking to my mother or Maryann, I was cutting young trees out of the huge chunk of Canadian Shield next to the house, grabbing and pulling and chopping as if I could free up the roots. It took me years to decide to wage war on the hodgepodge of growth on this great mound of stone—raspberry stalks and birch saplings and unrecognizable stuff with roots crawling underneath—years to care enough—because at the top of this rock, a huge metal cable leads up to a provincial hydro pole and a light that interferes with the stars.

But a month or so before, when a group of our friends were visiting, and a lot of wine and margaritas had been drunk, there was a contest with two ugly-looking slingshots to shoot out that light. Eventually, someone succeeded and, for the first time in all those years, the night was really night.

The thing about that light we shot out is that it went cold, then flickered, then somehow relit. There was nothing left—no discernible filament—but we got out the slingshots again. Would I go back in time? Would I call back the mother who danced in the kitchen or the brother who taught me to swim? What moment would I choose to relive? We cleaned up the broken glass and lay with our backs on the rock to take a good long look at the sky. Funny to think this piece of ground is the one I've known longest in my life and that Maryann's been in prison longer than I've been here.

41

That winter was going to be a tale of two cities: In Vancouver, my daughter Esta was pregnant with twins and the pregnancy was so precarious that she was confined to bed for several months. In Topeka, my mother was dying, but not so that anyone noticed. "I've been lazy today," she'd report. "But what could be nicer than lying here reading in bed?"

I went to see her.

I went to see my daughter. I came home and paced and wondered which one I should visit next. I was frightened. At such times, we want to make everything right, hold back the fates, put all the pieces together again. I was frightened, and instead of going to see my child or my mother, I went to see Maryann. Getting off the plane, I was actually not sure what I was doing there. The airport was almost empty. And the only motel room I could find had to be rented from a man who stood behind bulletproof glass. There were old Band-Aids in the shower; there was no phone. But I tried to compare my room with Maryann's cell as I pulled back the unpleasant bedspread and crawled in under it.

The next morning, the prison was exactly as I had left it, even to the stout woman at the desk at the visitors center. Same woman. Same giant scissors. "Are you wearing an underwire bra?" she asked, fully prepared to snip. Maryann had to be called away from work, but she was allowed to see me because I had come from so far away. The only other visitors were two women, elegant and well dressed. With them sat Leslie Van Houten, one of the three Manson girls. "I didn't know they were in prison with you. All this time and you never told me. Do you know them? What are they like? Do they stick together? How do the other women feel about them?" Yet again, I was stunned by Maryann's reticence. And how little I knew of her world! Leslie was very thin, with a long braid that was gray and a look of suffering stamped into her face.

It was a warm, overcast day and the prison, surrounded by those same thousands of cows, was blanketed by the smell of their shit. The stench was so overwhelming that I almost gagged. The visiting room was hot and there were hundreds of big buzzing flies. We pulled two plastic chairs up to a bench and sat facing each other, knee-to-knee, eye-to-eye. Immediately she asked about Esta. I said that a lot of people were actually praying for her. At a certain time. Every night. "We'll do that," Maryann told me. "We have a lot of stored-up energy in here." Then she smiled. "So you want to meet Leslie?" There was something challenging in her voice. I wondered if she might be jealous.

"Yes." I'd parked my rental car next to a new Lincoln that one of the visitors must have been driving.

"That's her mother. And a friend who brings her out here." Maryann was wearing the glasses I'd had an optometrist send down from Portland. I'd carried her prescription into a shop with Kristin, who'd also needed a new pair. I'd had to explain the situation, that I could not send them myself; it was against the rules. "They're for a woman in prison." It's interesting to see how people react to that. I'd asked one of the clerks to try them on because she looked a little like Maryann, if Maryann had been allowed to have bubbly hair and wear bright red lipstick.

When Leslie's visitors got up to leave, she came past us on her way out. In a minute, she would be strip-searched. Then she would go off to her job or back to her cell. But now Maryann introduced us, and Leslie gripped my hand, gazing at me with huge eyes and looking nothing like the young woman who'd carved an X on her forehead during her murder trial. "I've heard about you," she said.

I said I'd heard about her, as well.

I was going to have two days with Maryann—days when I should have been someplace else—and I hoped there would be time to talk about things we had not talked about before. We'd talked about the progress of her writ; whether she'd heard from her lawyer. We'd talked about her cellmate Valere, whose parole hearing was coming up. "She might get out this time."

"That will be like a divorce," I had told Maryann.

"Death," she had said.

We'd talked about William, about her father and mother, and now I said, "Did you ever get mad at them?"

"Just once," she said without stopping to think. "It was in Hawaii, during the trial. Dad had told me he had some money set aside. Money to help me if I really needed it. So one day this smooth lawyer named Winston Mirakitani finds me on a bench outside the courtroom. He's really short, but flashy in a white suit, and he says he can get me off for fifty thousand dollars. So I call Dad and he says he doesn't have the money. It was tied up in the Phoenix house. That made me really mad. But that's the only time."

"Couldn't he have sold it? I would have." I was sitting in a room buzzing with flies and heat and I told myself that my mother was simply old, simply fading, simply not feeling well, as she had been old and fading and not feeling well for three years. I told myself that Esta would be all right, that her twins would survive, and I crossed my fingers and leaned back in my chair. I said, "He could have mortgaged it."

She shook her head. "But he'd told the tenants they could have it for as long as they needed."

"You needed it more. He could have sold it to save you."

"He'd never go back on his word."

Judges 11:36: My father, if thou hast opened thy mouth unto the Lord, do to me according to that which hath proceeded out of thy mouth. "I got the box," I said, to change the subject. "How many thousands of pages did you send?" I had wanted to compare the court testimony Mike Brennan had sent Maryann to the words I'd written in my yellow notebook, but when a box half the size of a bathtub arrived, I'd more or less given up. Her lawyer had collected every extant page from the Hawaii trial—whatever had been kept by the prosecutor's office. Had I actually listened to all those millions and millions of words? Could anyone have made sense of them? Both Hioki and Futa had made William go over the most trivial details countless times, and every rehashing of events was slightly different. "He walked a little ways away from the car," William had said, describing Larry's murder. "And I told Maryann to watch him, but she indicated she could watch him from in the car. I instructed him to walk down to this little ravine. It wasn't the same place where Joe was. And I know when he walked down he's going to slip and fall. And before he gets back up the road, he won't know which way we turned." There were fifty versions of that paragraph. "I could see that he's going to slip and fall. He's not going to break his neck or nothing, but he's going to probably get scratched up."

What I noticed was how much I'd missed. I hadn't written a word about the forensics expert who testified that there were only two bullets and that Larry had been shot from behind.

William had stated many times that Maryann shot Larry three times while she was looking him in the face.

Another thing I hadn't mentioned in my notes was Bert Bray's testimony. Maryann's father had told us about talking to William in Yuma and persuading him to turn himself in. Had I listened? Had I wondered then, as I do now, why William went to Yuma instead of staying on the bus and trying to escape? And where was he during the intervening two days, while Maryann was languishing in jail?

"I didn't have anywhere to keep the box when Mike sent it," Maryann was saying.

"Did William ever drive your car?" I asked. "In Phoenix?"

"Yes. All the time. He'd come by to see me at work and ask for money."

"And that was a VW, but he said in court that he couldn't drive a stick shift."

"He could. He did. Definitely."

"Why would he bother with that little lie?" Mike Brennan and the students at USC were trying to prove that the state of Hawaii had depended on the testimony of a known informant, that the prosecutors had allowed him to perjure himself when he said he was serving life without parole, that they had not given Hioki accurate information about his California sentence. In one of his letters, William had written to Maryann, "Don't sweat it. You'll go free as I will not be believed and you will. I know this, and when you're out there, think of how I freed you. Think of the price you cost me." Even William believed himself to be unbelievable.

I noticed that another prisoner had come in to meet a visitor. "He comes all the time," Maryann said when I asked about them. I asked because they sat together like elderly couples sometimes sit, bowed over, with foreheads together, as if their moments together were measured and cherished.

"How old is she?"

"In her seventies, I guess. She killed an abuser. Not hers, though. Someone else's." The woman was small and delicately built. Her husband held her hand tenderly. That evening, Maryann was supposed to make a speech in front of the warden at a meeting of the Life Termers' Organization. She had recently been elected president and she took her duties seriously. Her speech would be about elderly prisoners, who cost the state an average of $66,000 a year. "There's a woman here on dialysis," she told me. "Has to go out to the hospital twice a week under guard. And do you have any idea what those guards get paid? A younger prisoner costs about twenty-eight thousand dollars to keep. That's a big difference. It's stupid to keep old women locked up. What harm are they going to do anybody?" Then she recited the statistic for lifers, which she knew by heart. Less than 1 percent come back once they're released. "We just don't come back. Our crimes are crimes of circumstance."

"Maryann," I said suddenly. "Let's find your birth mother."

"I told you she had me when she was sixteen?"

"Yes, you did. Yes. Your mother's exactly my age."

"And did I tell you it was my mother who left my father and me? He gave me up, but he did it out of love and wanting what was best for me. That's why I decided I wanted to know who he was. I'd been asking my mom questions about him, but she wouldn't tell me anything. Finally, I told her that no one could ever take her and Dad's place in my heart or my life, and she sent me a copy of the adoption papers."

"In here?"

"Yes. Containing my birth parents' names. Hers was Anna. His was Herbert. I was born Kerry Jean, which is kind of strange to think about."

"Why don't we—"

"I don't really have anyone left."

"You have Penne."

"Not quite."

"Pauline."

"But where is she?"

"Anna could still be alive."

"I know, but I don't care about her—especially after what my father told me. The last time he saw her was when he took her the divorce papers to sign. She was working in a bar. In Phoenix. Mother Anna." She looked away.

She was sixteen, I wanted to say. Try and remember yourself at that age. But I let it go. Included in the pages of testimony squeezed in the box were all the things we had not been allowed to hear—the bench conferences between the judge and the attorneys and his instructions to them. Hioki had kept trying to prevent things. That was his tactic, but he didn't seem to know what he was up against.

"Then what happened?"

"She shot him, shot him."

"How many times?"

"Three."

I told Maryann I would see her in the morning, and I went out slowly, with nothing to do for the rest of the night but read more pages of testimony. I had brought a stack in my suitcase. The parking lot was empty, and when I climbed the three steps to the visitors center to retrieve my car key, the keeper handed them over, she of the scissors. But when I put the key in the car lock, the car alarm went off and I glanced quickly up at the guard towers, where there were guns trained on me.

42

Saturdays at the prison are busy. This one had the usual young fathers holding babies, and grandmothers with older children or other relatives. A father gave his infant a bottle without looking at her, then held her up on his shoulder and slapped at her back, saying, "Good girl, good girl." Another cycle, I thought.

The scissor lady at the visitors center had smiled at me. The day before, she had helped me call the car-rental place, and they had told me to use the button on my keypad instead of the key. I had not been shot or arrested and I had found a nicer place to sleep. Today, we could sit outside, where the flies were less pestering and where there were more things to be seen. A mother and daughter whispering to each other in Spanish. And a prisoner named Anika, who was from Sweden. "She just wants to go home, but California won't let her," Maryanne told me.

I also met Pat, another Manson girl, who told me she read

every book that I sent Maryann. Pat's mother was visiting in a wheelchair and they sat together for several hours, their two heads bent.

"How was the speech last night?"

"It went great. I was nervous having the warden right there in front of me, but he seemed impressed with my research."

The usual moment of disinclination overwhelmed me. My mother. My child. Why was I here instead of there? "Maryann, in court William mentioned other robberies. He told the arresting officer in L.A. that there were several in both California and Hawaii."

"In California, yes. But not in Hawaii."

"You're sure? Why would he say that?"

"I don't know."

"Why didn't you disagree?"

"They never asked me."

"True. Hioki dropped the ball a hundred times. But why didn't they interview you in California?"

"Because"—she lowered her gaze—"I wouldn't talk to them without my lawyer and he wouldn't give them anything without a deal."

I muttered, "Meanwhile, they gave William the sweetest deal of his life. But William said you did one robbery alone." I was looking through her new glasses and into her eyes, which were suddenly wet. "Tell me."

Maryann nodded. She said that on June 25, while Larry Hasker's body was being identified in Hawaii, she had acted as lookout while William robbed a store in Downey, California. The next day, in Bellflower, she went into a U-Totem store, pulled a gun out of her purse, threatened the clerk, and took the money in the till while William waited in Cesario Arauza's stolen car. "And that woman had a breakdown. She'd been robbed before two times and she ended up in a mental hospital." A pause. "I did that to her. I took that piece of her life. I mean, she went home again, back to her kids, but I did that.

The others were different, but that one was mine. . . . And why didn't I just tell her to call the cops, that there was a lunatic in the car outside? I could have, should have, told the clerk what was happening and had her call the police. But I was still doing what Bill told me to do."

"Did you use the gun?"

"I had it."

"Tell me about when you got picked up by Cesario Arauza. Because I have a theory. You can tell me if it makes sense."

"We started hitchhiking. To northern California," she said quietly. "I think it was the same day we landed in L.A., but I'm not sure anymore. Then we were coming back down."

"So Cesario picked you up and William was sitting in back."

"We had been riding with him for several hours when William pulled the gun on him and told him to pull off to the side. The man didn't have that much money on him. I don't know what William had in his mind."

"And he was nice to you."

"Who?"

"Cesario. In his testimony, William said you stopped someplace and tried to leave without him, the two of you." The words William had used were elaborate, like my one-horned goat. He'd said, "They wanted to throw me out and keep going, and there's a lot of ramifications as to why it happened. You know, it went over and over and over and over and over. And it was a senseless thing, and it happened, you know."

"We never stopped until William told him to. Then they got out and walked down an embankment and I heard the gunshots."

Was it possible that the whole scenario about the gas station and the ten dollars and the lunch was invented? "He said Cesario made a pass at you. Or that's what you told him. Maybe he thought you were planning to go off together. The way you were going off with Larry Hasker after you dropped William at the apartment."

"But that was William's idea. That's what he told Larry when he asked him for a ride home."

"Because Larry was coming on to you. But Joe Leach was different. He was a lot older than William. Forty something. And he never really tried anything, did he? And those were the only three people you and William were ever alone with. Am I right? Larry and Cesario were your age. They were young. Younger than William. He thought they were coming on to you. Remember how William described Cesario? I just read it again in the testimony. 'He was bigger. A lot bigger.' Surely someone in the last twenty or so years must have suggested this. Someone must have thought of jealousy as a motive."

"I never thought of that," Maryann said, although she always describes her ex-husband as possessive, controlling. "He said that he got messages, that killing Arauza was part of a plan. And after he killed Larry Hasker, he said it was something he had to do. He said I wouldn't understand. He got in the car and told me to go. He was very calm and matter-of-fact."

"So control was a huge part of his reality."

"It was always there. I was always being tested. He'd say, 'What did I tell you yesterday?' And I'd have to recite it."

Stand up straight. What did I tell you? Spell spaghetti. *Now.*

"I was one hundred percent positive that he wouldn't hesitate to kill me if I went against him. But the next day, I did tell him I wanted to go home, and he told me he couldn't allow that because he couldn't go back to prison and I'd turn him in. So we came back to L.A. Together on the same plane."

"Couldn't you have found a way to—"

"Up in Merced one night when we were there, he drank a lot and seemingly passed out, so when he didn't wake up, I got out of bed, got dressed, grabbed a twenty-dollar bill. He usually would wake up and even follow me to the bathroom in the middle of the night to make sure I didn't leave, so now I was going to get as far away as I could. I ran to the bus station. It was two o'clock in the morning and the station was closed. I found out it wouldn't be open until six or seven, and I was trying to figure out where to go, when Bill came up behind me and, with the gun in my ribs, asked me where I thought I was going. The next day, we started hitchhiking back south and got picked up by Cesario."

Another what-if.

The night Maryann was arrested in Long Beach, William had asked her to go out and get some cigarettes. He'd given her the car keys. He'd let her out of his sight for the first time since the Joe Leach robbery. But minutes later, she was pulled over by the police. Had he called them? "Bill had pulled a robbery earlier that night, so maybe the car was identified. They detained me for quite a while on the street and then they got a team together and stormed the motel, but Bill was gone and they arrested me. Initially, it was only the robberies, but later they charged me with murder."

Maryann's husband had left the case for her glasses in the room, and in it there were four bullets, all hollow points. Then, while she was taken off to jail, he got himself down to Yuma. And how did Maryann's father manage not to strangle his son-in-law? Instead, they sat in the living room drinking ginger ale and fingering paper napkins until William got up and paced back and forth, wired and volatile. He had come for help, and he finally agreed to let Bert call the sheriff. "But can I have some breakfast first?"

"He had a thing about my dad," Maryann said. "He used to call him all the time from jail. Collect, you know. And when my mom answered, she'd just hang up. But Dad would take the call."

"My father used to say he would never bail me out if I went to jail."

"Were you ever mad at him?"

"I never got as far as that. Just scared. But I was mad at my mother once."

"My dad took those calls out of love," said Maryann proudly, and we moved from that to the love so evident all around us . . . the sight of these relatives and friends, of these church mentors and pen pals and strangers going through the loops, taking the time: the husband who comes week after week, year after year. The mother. The teenager in a black hooded sweatshirt, pulling the hood up around his face and then letting it down. Even the evident affection between Maryann and Anika, between Maryann and Pat. Her tone when she mentioned Valere . . . "We went to dinner last night because they were serving something edible." And the story of Valere eating all the fudge Maryann had made in the immersion pot. "I said, Don't you want your cocoa and chocolate pudding, too?"

Then, "What was it with your mother?" Maryann asked. "When you got mad."

"She told me to give up a certain boy."

Maryann looked straight at me. Then she laughed. "Lucky you."

43

Now, when it is too late, I remember Maryann telling me her two regrets. The first one was William. The other one was not being with her parents when they were dying. Next to my desk there are two photographs of my mother. One, taken in her early thirties, is the face I gazed at from my crib or from my high chair or even from her lap, although I don't remember her ever holding me. This photograph is an enlargement that Michael and Kristin made for the funeral. They also enlarged the other one, taken at the lunch to celebrate her ninetieth birthday, where she is holding up an icy glass of vodka and looking bemused by all of us. We had gathered to celebrate a birthday she could not accept. We had bullied her out of her bed and up onto her feet. We had dressed her in creamy silk and put a corsage on her breast. We had come from hither and yon, from the now and the past, and we had made a party for her with all the love that she had given us. Sometimes I look at the second picture and sometimes at the first. They are both my mother. Since her death, I seem to have fallen in love with her, along with my brand-new granddaughter, as if I am a link between what is gone and what is to come. How not to think of the baby given away during a courthouse lunch break. Unwanted babies and babies who represent life.

By the time we got to Topeka, my mother was lying on a steel table in the storage room of a funeral home. She was cold, having been in a freezer. I had told them not to touch her. I did not want her embalmed.

Kristin and I went in with a paper bag. Is all grief more or less the same? Ask Mr. and Mrs. Hasker, who did not have the satisfaction of a finished life. Ask Maryann, who lives on both ends of it. The bag held a silk dress, a pair of stockings, earrings, and the Fabergé egg she liked to wear on a chain.

Someone closed the door behind us.

Mother was naked, covered with a sheet. Her hair had been washed a few days before but had lost its set. Falling back from her face as she lay on that table, it was longer than usual, and her beautiful nose was more hooked, the nostrils open and dark. Her mouth was drawn back. Here was flesh pared down, as if carved by a careful knife. Mother used to say, "I don't know who will see me dead. I worry about this." But as Kristin and I combed her hair and washed her face and thought about what underwear she would want—All of it? But that was so much, too much—we both cried as we talked to her. A ruby red slip. Panties. Stockings: the old-fashioned kind in two separate pieces. (We had found a pair ready, in her bureau. Who put them there? She always wore the other kind.) A touch of lipstick. Her silver earrings. So that here is my mother stretched out in her purple dress and when I am alone with her, I can climb on the table and bury my face in her breast as I never could do in her air-breathing life. I can open her lips to pour her last pleasure of vodka between them. I can open her eyes and rub my tears into them, flakes of anger washed away.

I know she will do as she has always done: wait for my father, who is late, for my brother, who is gone, for her comforts, which are private, and her long death, which is begun.

Because of the funeral, I was late getting to Vancouver, but I arrived a few hours before the twins were born. Two months early. Elliott, the littlest one, did not survive.

As a family, we are shaken to the bones. Have known death and birth and death. Have grieved and rejoiced and grieved. Sometimes now, I lie half-awake for fifteen or twenty minutes in the morning, having dreamed that I am not in a coffin, but in prison. Worrying up the details. That watching of clocks. On the one hand, time stretches out like those railroad tracks in pictures that describe infinity. But the other clock, the one that lives in our bodies, ticks faster and faster. I am going to die and never get out. I imagine that as an old woman I'll take to my bed and live like this, in the half-light, exactly as my mother did at the end. "There may come a day," she would say, "when I just refuse to get up. Like the old aunt did in Proust."

Only when a nurse forced her into the shower and down to the hairdresser did she decide she had really had enough.

Of course I am grateful to this nurse, as I am grateful to every single one of the good people who took care of my mother over the last two years of her life. Would that I had done it all! I felt so heroic, so necessary, when I flew into Kansas City, rented a car, drove to Topeka, and stumbled into my mother's apartment—the place I had foisted on her. Usually, I found her in bed. Usually, it was time for lunch. "You're not dressed!" I'd bark at her before we had managed our usual furtive kiss.

"Oh well, I thought you'd have eaten. I didn't know what time you'd be here."

"But you! It's lunchtime for you. I could smell the food downstairs when I came in."

"Oh well. I've had something."

"Such as what?" I actually liked the food downstairs. For some idiotic reason, eating in this dining room always cheered me up. It made me feel young, vital, and compassionate. I took an interest in each old face, each trembling conversation. I leaned into the space between the tables the better to eavesdrop. There were moments when I wanted to embrace every resident. I loved the staff. Once, when Kristin and I were visiting together, we asked for a meeting with them to discuss Mother's lethargy. Mother came to the meeting with us. We said we were becoming really worried. She had given up on the exercise class in the morning and there was the new tendency not to eat. They had turned off her stove after she sent billows of smoke down the hall. That was awful, like having to give up her car. She had a toaster oven, but she kept trying to make toast on the heating pad of the coffeepot. She cooked her eggs in the water as it slowly heated up. What should we do?

The director told Mother that she should go to the exercise class. "Oh my," said Mother coyly. "I had no idea. Why of course I'll go. What time is it, did you say?" She had always complained about the early hour of this class, but now she smiled and said, "Fine. Fine," and I knew, all over again, how she had lived her life. The promise was a polite fabrication. It was a recipe for survival, a way to keep us at bay. She had defended my father, dead now for thirty-two years. She had been stylish and witty and charming and smart. She had kept her chin up when my brother's death had mangled her heart. She had learned to speak Spanish; she liked to conjugate. She had made elegant meals. She had knit and embroidered and sewn and created exquisite decoupage boxes and eggs. She had entertained the Ballets Russes and made light of my obvious failings. She had taken care of me, of my cats and dogs and fish. With her bare hands. Even when they were arthritic. She had tended my children. She had said, "When you feel envy and wish you were someone else, remember that you have to take the whole life."

Even when I rebelled against her, my mother was the center of what I did. See how I put my feet on the table in my own house? See how I dance, how I write books, how I fly to Europe, how I live in sin? There was a need to shock, but there was another, stronger need, as well. I have longed to live in my mother's image.

She was younger than I am when she became a widow. Then she survived for another thirty-two years. In that time, she learned to manage my father's small pension and the few stocks left to her. She sold the big house and moved into a tiny one two blocks away and seemed not to look back, although she dreamed, she said, only of the larger house, the place she had created in her prime. Because she lived those years so very well, I have my map to a good old age. Yes, I see it coming and it cannot frighten me. I feel her legs in my legs, her back in my back. I go to the kitchen to make coffee and remember that she always readied hers before she went to bed. Soon I will do the same. We do not practice age. It is performed for us. In our retrieval of those things as we grow old, we capture the people we have loved. Contain them once they are lost.

44

Maybe I liked flying down to Corona, jumping in a rented car, and arriving at the prison with my good cheer and health intact, the way I liked flying down to my mother when she was still within reach. Maybe I liked knowing that neither Mother nor Maryann could get up and follow me. I was in charge.

But when Maryann describes her life, she talks about the jobs she's held and her two-year college degree. Her accomplishments feel as real to her as mine do to me. She sent me a basket she'd made out of pine needles, although acquiring the materials took weeks. She reads books on tape for blind students. She belongs to organizations that manage to do things for people outside. So when she learned that her sister had cancer, she was stunned, then hurt, then angry; she felt cut off and betrayed. Penne had known for three years. She'd been through three surgeries, chemotherapy, and the usual dose of fear, but

Maryann had never been told. Then Penne had sent a form letter, something she sent out in duplicate to everyone on her list. "It was along the lines of finding out I had a great-nephew when he was three years old," Maryann wrote to me. "It's like I don't count as close-enough family to share these little tidbits with." The flash of sarcasm was a signal of anger; I had learned that much. But, when the anger passed, she thought about Penne being the last of her family. She had not let Maryann call her for several years, saying it ran up her phone bill, but she had been out there—someone in the world who had known Maryann from the very beginning. "I wonder if I'll make it out of here in time to see her and spend some time with her. Even though we haven't been the closest of sisters, I don't like the thought of losing my whole family while I'm in here!"

It was impossible to write back to her dying sister. So much had gone unsaid between them and so much had already been said. Maryann put the letter away, feeling it was too late. At the time of their parents' fiftieth wedding anniversary, she had asked her father on the phone if anyone was going to throw a party. He had sounded rueful. "No one to do that but Penne," he'd said. "And you and I know that's doubtful." Maryann had contacted Penne and suggested that they do something to mark the event. "I can't do much in here," she had written, "but I saw a cross-stitch sampler I'd like to do and maybe you could help." At that point, Penne had rallied. And in 1992, when she read about William's confession in *California Legal Magazine,* it was Penne who contacted Deborah Fraser about the confession and then helped Fraser worry up legal and historical details. This was something; this was almost good. But when Gladys got sick, Penne abandoned Maryann. "She said there was a bank account with my name on it and that she was in charge of it. She said the Phoenix house was mine; they'd left it to me. But she won't give me anything in writing. I guess she's always been jealous of me in a lot of ways. My logical mind says she didn't tell me about her cancer because she didn't want me to worry, but another part wants to let her know how I felt like she still doesn't accept me as her sister and that I just really don't matter to her. She was always saying 'my mom this and my dad that' and I'd have to tell her they were my parents too. And the will. I've never seen it. I don't know what's in the bank account. Maybe nothing. She won't tell me."

In my answer, I told Maryann about my mother's brown suitcase. How she had been proud of it—stylish and round, with a long, looped strap. I said she had used it, over the last years of her life, to store a collection of letters my father had written to her during the war. Once, I had asked if I could read them. He was my father. I had no similar pile of letters from him, not even one letter to keep in a private drawer. My mother had made a strange sound, like something coming from far away. They were sent to her, she'd told me flatly. Her alone. What's more, she'd taken scissors to them so I would never read certain words.

Scissors.

I promised myself that I would read what was left of those wartime letters the minute my mother died. When she moved to the shiny new apartment, I shoved the round suitcase under her bed and tapped it with a hand or a foot whenever I went to see her. On each visit, I slid it an inch or two farther under the bed, so she would not notice it. The day would come, I told myself, when it would not matter if I opened the suitcase and read those letters. I wanted to learn how he spoke to her, how he thought about things, how he expressed himself when he was different.

There must have been such a time.

A few weeks later, when Maryann called to tell me Penne was dead, I couldn't believe it. Then I realized Penne had never been real. Not to me. After all our letters and conversations, I still didn't believe that Maryann had a life or a story beyond the walls of the prison. "Oh dear God," I said, and I meant it, because Maryann would never have a chance to make things right with Penne now. This sister who refused her phone calls. This sister who sent her a form letter explaining her terminal disease. This sister who had better things to do than visit an inmate. "Will you send flowers for me?" the inmate asked. "There's no way to do it from in here."

45

Of course summer, as usual, followed that wild spring. We went back up to the cottage as we have always done. When I got phone calls from Maryann, I didn't remind her that our correspondence had been going on for three years, that this was a kind of anniversary, that three years before, her attorney had been about to reopen her case. He had filed a writ of habeas corpus in Hawaii. Delays and more delays. Postponements. I didn't tell her that I should have gone to Topeka instead of Corona, that I will regret that decision for the rest of my life.

She told me she'd dreamed she called home to talk to her father and that Governor Davis answered the phone. Maryann asked him why he wouldn't let anyone out of prison when so many women deserved to be released. And how could he visit her father and yet deny him the chance to spend his last years with her?

I told her I'd called Larry Hasker's father. "I said I might want to write about the murder and about your case and asked if he would tell me about Larry. I wanted to know about his childhood, about his personality, about his hopes and dreams, because it seems wrong to leave him out of your story."

For a few seconds, Maryann didn't say anything. Then she said, "What happened?"

"With Mr. Hasker? Well, he didn't want to talk to me about Larry if I was writing a book about you." Then I said I had tried to find Kimberly, Larry's sister. In the courtroom, she was just a girl, a sister, someone who had been called to testify. But later, in my mind, she became a person with unbearable grief. That was after I knew what it was to lose a brother, although it was a grief I could never describe. A brother is a piece of your flesh—arm, leg, DNA. Same parents. Same secrets. A brother is your image in the mirror.

I said, "Kimberly seems to have disappeared."

Maryann said it was hot in the prison, and I told her that I was about to jump in the river. Why protect her from the truth of my life? My hands were dirty. I'd been planting a stargazer lily in a place where it would stand out and be noticed. I told her I had visions of a more civilized landscape—a bush here, a clump of flowers there. I had a brand-new granddaughter to think about. Since Gemma's birth and my mother's death, I could see my life played out on this landscape. Beginning, middle, end—it has definite shape. But what does a person do without such a set of rocks and trees, board and roof? I was still reading through the pages of testimony Maryann had sent. They included the actual plea agreement William had signed with Charles Marsland, the aggrieved DA. Jan Futa's name was there, as well. Another set of papers in the box involved jailhouse informants. There was a scandal and it had hit the newspapers. In 1988, the L.A. district attorney announced that no more jailhouse informants were to be used as witnesses.

William was never mentioned in the article, but he was gone by then, practicing his trade in other states.

When I drove off to our little town with its one clothing store, one drugstore, one grocery store, it was because Maryann had asked me to send her a quarterly box. Sheron was sick and there was no one else, so I told Maryann it would be a pleasure to send the thirty pounds of candy and nuts and the packets of dried tuna and tea and coffee she was allowed to receive four times a year, although the denim shorts she needed were required to have an eleven-inch inseam and they might be hard to find in our summer town with its one small shop.

In California, there was about to be a recall of Governor Davis. This was not because he had agreed to parole only six lifers, in all his years in office, while the parole board had recommended the release of 285. Instead, he was accused of abusing state funds. In Texas, the Democrats had gone into hiding in order to prevent a vote that would redistribute legislative districts and thereby give Republicans a decisive majority in Congress. In Hawaii, there was going to be a conference call with Maryann's lawyer. Jan Futa was supposed to have readied her argument. Or would she delay again?

At the prison, the warden had invited a few people from a program called Canine Service Training in for a tour. Not only did they come, inspecting cells, yards, and prisoners; they also brought four dogs along with them. The dogs were trained to help people with disabilities. Some of the trainers were nuns. The morning of the tour, Maryann had gone to work and someone mentioned the visiting dogs. Maryann looked at her boss, who said, "Oh, go on!" and she found the dogs in front of her housing unit, along with their trainers, the warden, several administrators, and a number of lifers, who hadn't been close to a dog in twenty or thirty years. The nuns were allowing them to pet the dogs and some of the women were crying. All of this had an impact on the warden, who decided that CIW should participate in the program. A few of the inmates would have puppies to train.

"You love animals," I said when Maryann told me the story.

Maryann said, "But what if I get called out to court in Hawaii?"

I teased her about not being able to commit when she was serving a life sentence. I said it was the way her father had been when he came home from the war. Paralyzed. I said, "If you get called, you'll go. You have to let them see you. Represent yourself. But you still sign up for a dog."

She answered quickly. "If I go out of here, even for a night, I lose my room. I lose my roommate and my neighbors in the unit. If I don't have to go, I won't. Still, I'm not ready for a dog. It's too much responsibility."

That summer, along with phone calls from Maryann, I had an invitation from my old Topeka girlfriends, who were going to get together for several days on a lake in Minnesota. It would be our first glimpse of one another in more than forty years, since none of them had gone to the high school reunion. Most of us had gone to nursery school together. We had lived within a few blocks of one another. Our mothers were our Scout leaders and had something called the Mothers' Group, while among the daughters, relationships varied in intensity over the years. All through grade school, I was closest to Joyce, who lost her hearing in the fifth grade. Would she mind my telling this? No, it is one of the things that has defined her life. Another is her Jewish family, therefore her difference from the rest of us. Growing up, I thought it was exciting that they had no Christmas tree, that the four daughters received gifts for eight consecutive nights. I thought it was miraculous that she learned to read lips so I could talk to her silently from across the room.

In high school, I was closest to Wendy, who lived in the house behind mine. We shared double dates with two boys who were best friends. The car, the drive-in movies, the path between our houses, the phone every night. Joyce, Wendy, and the rest of them would be together in Minnesota, and the thought of it terrified me. The rest of them had kept in contact. The rest of them had seen one another here or there or somewhere in between. The rest of them knew about husbands and children and parents. Who had been born, who had died. These childhood friends would still be married to their original husbands. Would have lived normal lives. They had never burned bridges. What did we now have in common? We had known one another's parents: the mothers who stayed home except when they went to the beauty shop or the grocery store; the fathers who drove off in new-model American cars every morning and who were each and every one Republican to the core except for mine, who stood out with his old car, his liberal views, and his returns from the office at midnight. I wondered how Maryann would feel about meeting old friends again. For three years, I'd wanted to go back with her to Honolulu. I had pictured her there, running down those courthouse steps, as if all the stories I'd read and all the movies I'd seen and all the TV shows I'd watched were promises of what could really happen. It had seemed significant that her lawyer decided to reopen the Hawaii case the week I first wrote to her—as if something was pulling us together. I had wanted to be a mirror for her, but it was working in reverse. Given a chance like this reunion, wouldn't I want Maryann to say yes?

I found a pair of denim shorts in our country store. I had brought a tape measure. I tried to forget about Mr. Hasker, his bitterness, his ache. And Kimberly. For an entire week, the quarterly box and the invitation kept my mind elsewhere.

46

"Why didn't you ever answer my letters?" Wendy asked. "Didn't you know that I loved you?"

"After Mexico," said Joyce, "I never saw you again. We were so close. I was closer to you than to anyone else in my life."

I did my best to explain, but I noticed that much of the time I spent with my childhood friends in Minnesota was concerned with our mothers.

All being dead but three.

Liz's mother, in fact, drove over to see us and stayed for a glass of champagne. She was alert, interested in each of us, and stimulating. Sitting gracefully in her chair with her ankles crossed, wearing stockings and small heels, wearing jewelry that suited her and attractive clothes—pants and a silk shirt— she made me ache. We all felt the same. We hovered around Liz's mother and drank in her intelligence, her questions and opinions. Mulled wine, she was, to our motherless bodies.

So here we are, tending our mothers in memory or in the flesh, my own most intimate moments with my mother having occurred after her death. I cannot really tell my friends about this, although without those minutes in the basement of the funeral home, I would never have recognized my terrible need. Instead, we talk about living mothers, the ones who are left. We talk about their depressions, their housing, the long, curled toenails on arthritic feet. How much are we willing to give of ourselves to our parents? How angry or selfish are we? How much do we still resent the old brutalities and withheld faith? Someone says that being a grandmother will change me. I will finally see another person uncritically. I will give up my investment in judging. I have to smile at that, since I missed or gave up the one real chance I had.

It's odd, but we are not much interested in talking about our children during these magical four days. What we have in common is our own childhoods and the secrets we never shared back then and the secrets we didn't even know we had. Because we grew up in Topeka, we talk about the famous Supreme Court case that bears its name and what it meant to them and to me. *Brown vs. Board of Education of Topeka, Kansas.* SCHOOL SEGREGATION BANNED, the headlines had read back in 1954. And now, sitting on folding chairs by a Minnesota lake, someone says, "But in fifth grade, we already had Alice and Fanny in our school."

I say that was because my father was president of the school board. How could they not have realized? And suddenly I'm thinking, What a father! He ran for the school board because I couldn't spell. He ran because he wanted to restore the teaching of phonics to our schools. He wanted the best public education possible for me. For everyone. Then he got embroiled in school board politics. He wanted teachers to be promoted according to merit, and that enraged the teachers' union. Most of the teachers turned against him. They were about to build a school on a floodplain that belonged to someone powerful and rich—

another dangerous enemy. My father stopped the contract. There were threats, a lawsuit. It was a scandal. And when the Browns sued the school board because their daughter was refused admission to a certain public school, my father said the Browns were right. Schools that were separate facilities could not, by definition, be equal. And equality of opportunity is what the U.S. Constitution guaranteed.

As a ten-year-old, I had no idea that the Supreme Court decision was going to change the world. What I knew was that my father was never home, was always at meetings, was more and more volatile. He was losing friends and clients. There were stores we didn't enter, people my parents wouldn't see. People who, if glimpsed, caused us to cross the street. There were children I didn't play with anymore. Teachers who didn't like me. I kept getting in fights and being sent to the principal's office.

If Topeka decided to integrate the schools, as my father wished, should the board still defend itself at the Supreme Court, or should it drop out of the case? For the first time, school board meetings were open to the public. My father wanted the town to decide for itself to do what was right, but he wanted the Supreme Court to establish a precedent. He wanted the case to be heard and won by the Browns and he wanted Topeka to be a model for everyone else. It was an odd fence to straddle, but he managed to straddle it, starting the process of desegregation with my classroom on the privileged side of town, a year before the decision, so there would be less argument. Linda Brown's school would have to wait.

I remember a cross being burned in our yard, although it must have been a bad dream. And the phone calls at dinnertime. Communist. Nigger-lover. Wait till your daughter marries one. I heard my father get up in the middle of the night. His back pains were chronic. He had a workbench in the garage, and he'd go out there while Mother and I slept. Under a single bulb in the garage ceiling, he'd work on the sailboat, although he never managed, after that year, to put it back in the lake. In the morning, he would rush off to his law practice, but he grew more and more exhausted, more and more short-tempered, and I began to hide when I saw him coming.

Up to the bathroom again, where I locked the door.

But now, telling the story to my friends, it begins to make sense.

That long-ago year, I had two best friends. Joyce was one of them and Alice Smith was the other. Alice was accomplished in all sorts of ways that were new to me. She hit home runs at recess and rode her bike without touching the handlebars. She was full of jokes and good at arithmetic. I'd never known a black person before, except for our cleaning lady, but Alice was convincing proof that ability had nothing to do with race. Secretly, I felt a certain pride in her accomplishments, knowing that my father had given Alice to our school.

Looking back on it from this distance, my father seems to have struggled for something that would have happened any-way, but maybe there is more to it than that. In a pile of papers in Mother's house, I found the old news clippings about *Brown vs. Board of Education* and read enough to understand the part my father had played in an important piece of history. He was thirty-nine years old when he was elected to the school board and he died seventeen years after Linda Brown won her case. Hard years. Years that drained the joy out of his life. He was never made a judge, as he should have been. But what my father did was deliver a cogent plan for desegregating schools that helped Topeka do what was right before it was ordered to do so. And while he was at it, he gave the Browns room to win their case so that desegregation was, at last, guaranteed.

To think he had run for election in the first place because I couldn't spell.

The news clippings were part of a mess of papers I found in my mother's house when I was going through everything after she died. I also found the single-spaced instruction sheet I was given before the mock trial about the goat—the trial I had a role in at the law school, acting as a witness, knees together and back straight. At the bottom of the first page it says "Return this script to the Dean's office after the trial," as if it were to be held in strictest confidence.

As it turned out, the injured party in the mock trial was not a goat, but a little boy. The boy's arm was broken. There was a car involved and a goat, too, but the goat was unharmed. Not so my father. Among the papers was a manila envelope full of letters from various doctors and certain close friends and associates. They were written to the Internal Revenue Service because my father had not paid his taxes for several years. Many years. Each of the letters said, in one way or another, that my father's mental health during the decade before his death was deteriorating. Along with his friends, medical professionals testified—doctors and psychiatrists—that my father was clinically depressed. They put the start of his condition at about the time of the Topeka tornado in 1966, when a company he had invested in was badly hit. He had put all our money into this business, trying to save it for one of his clients. He had put other people's money in, as well, although he should not have done that. Without enough insurance, the damage should have meant the end, but my father took out further loans and cashed in his life insurance. He did not want the men at the plant to be out of work. He could not lose the money he'd put into the company or the money he had borrowed from other clients. Who knows what else was at stake? The letters were written after his death because my mother had been left nearly penniless and the IRS was going to make her pay.

I probably shook my head, sitting there on the floor reading those letters, because I knew that the condition they described had started much earlier—years before the tornado in 1966. "Spell *precipitous*," he'd say, snapping his fingers. "And look at me." When he was angry, I had to remember to answer, "yes, sir." My resistance was physical. But at the first choked sob, my father would become furious. "I'll give you something to cry about." This temper, this lack of patience, this chronic irritability came home with my father from the war—that's what I think—the way Bert's indecision and paralysis came home with him. The Topeka school board may have broken him, but my guess is that when my father got out of the Studebaker that day in 1945 and was told that he'd have to get the ladder out of the garage and climb up to the second-floor bathroom window to see his two-year-old daughter, who'd locked herself up deliberately, he felt the first prickling of rage. He had come from the train station, where my mother had gone to pick him up. He had climbed out of the car and, because of the injury to his back, because of jumping down to the ground from that troop plane in Honolulu and then reaching up to catch his bag, he must have limped as he walked up the driveway. I can see my brother running out of the house and grabbing his father around the waist, so happy to see him after that long year away. He's been watching from the front-room window or even crouching by the bushes outside. "Linda's locked herself in the bathroom," he says, and my father, who will never again sleep painlessly through a night, has to fetch the ladder and lean it against the side of the house he has tried to defend with his life.

47

There is also this. I'm in the backseat of my father's car with Joyce. He's put his best hat on the seat and tells us not to touch it, but we are suffering from excitement, driving to Kansas City to see the Ice Capades. We are jumping around, pinching and tickling and laughing, and the outcome is clear. I see us pulling up at the curb in front of my grandmother's house to take her along with us. I see us still giggling as my father opens our door and spies his hat. We notice it, too, squashed, beyond repair, beyond ever wearing again, and I know this will be the end of everything—the wonderful Ice Capades, the dinner out, the sleepover at my grandmother's house. Even in front of Joyce, who, of all my friends, is my father's favorite, the happiness we've brought with us from Topeka will collapse. All the silliness disappears. We watch him brush off the hat, push at its crown, look at us for a moment, and smile. Then he laughs.

"I used to go to the Ice Capades," Maryann says when I tell her this story. And then I decide to go see her again and this time meet Valere. Because how can I know Maryann unless I know the cell mate who probably knows her better than she knows herself? Friends are like that. They give us context. And I will have to go with a friend of my own, because only one prisoner is allowed per visitor. Susie lives in northern California and she agrees to apply for approval to visit the prison as long as we can make the entire trip in one day. She has a ranch: animals to look after. So we fly.

Down south, the cows are sadder than ever, but the day is cool, and where there is grass, it's green. Susie can see the guard tower looming over the vast herds, and I tell her there are sixteen hundred women on the human side of the fence. Having a companion along offers me a new set of eyes. I can see that those of us who are waiting outside the prison look exactly like any group clustered anyplace. We are quiet. We are variously dressed. What is unusual is our patience. The grandparents with youngsters never flinch at the flies or dust. When we get inside, we can see the people who are already lucky enough to have been reunited behind the glass. They're sitting in clusters and visiting the vending machines, and by 4:00 p.m., we're beginning to make jokes about the empty slots that will be left for us. "Yesterday they refilled them," someone says.

There is a slight sense of collegiality, but it is slight.

What we can see through the soundproof glass is only a tiny percentage of the two million Americans who live in prisons, but, even so, Susie is astonished. "It's not even two million," I tell her. "It's more than that. Since I started writing to Maryann, another two hundred thousand people have been sent to jails. She more or less keeps me up-to-date." I tell Susie that her state built San Quentin first, and then, in the next hundred years, only eight more prisons got built. But during the eight years Ronald Reagan was president, nine big prisons were built in his state. So much damage. So much harm. The death penalty was resumed. Then twelve more prisons were built. One person out of every 138 lives in one of them. "It's a business," I say. "Not just in California but all over the States. Some are privately owned. They turn a huge profit. The corporations that own them lobby for longer sentences and tighter laws because they make money off of every inmate."

"How?"

"Contracts. They're paid by the head. Like for cows."

In the outside waiting area, three people are talking about the need for stricter and longer punishment. "They're someone's family?" Susie sounds horrified, but by the time we meet Maryann and Valere, we have set politics aside. We are just four women getting our food, warming it up in the microwave, making the kind of small talk any four women might make. Rain has begun outside, so we bring in the last four available plastic chairs, dry them off, and sit. I'm happy to see Maryann. I no longer tell myself that I am the reason she is here. She is someone to whom I owe something, but there is more to it than that: I care about her. And there is a feeling in the room brought on by the outside rain, by the long wait, by the reunited families. As a foursome, we seem to be able to say anything. "Tell us about the strip searches. Who does them? The wardens?" Susie points to a woman in uniform with the usual weapons around her middle.

"Those are COs. The old ones were okay. But now because of Schwarzenegger, they all want to retire, and the new batch is overtrained. They're always just itching for something to happen."

"For what kind of things?"

"Fights," Valere says. "Yesterday, they used pepper spray."

Maryann says, "It gives them a chance to strip-search us again, look for scratches or something with their flashlights."

"Do you believe her?" Susie had asked me on the plane. "I mean, is she innocent?" I had said, "How can I ever know."

It was my usual defense. "What do we really know about any-one? Even on a jury, all you have is the offered evidence," Susie said. "But this is real life." Normally, any four women I'd be chatting with over tacos and burritos might discuss a thing like strip searches done to women in prison, but normally none of us would have experienced such a thing. On the other hand, if Valere and Maryann share our outrage, they've learned to live with it. It might be bravery or it might be something different, something I know no name for yet. Valere says Maryann is most notable for this stoicism, since she's served twenty-six years for two murders she didn't do. "I took a life," Valere says. "I deserved to do time."

"But why do you think so? What about the battered-woman argument? Maryann says he beat you up all the time."

"I killed someone. I was doing drugs at the time. I probably wouldn't have done it otherwise."

"You didn't set out to kill him," Maryann puts in. "And he was one mean son of a bitch."

We laugh. Susie is dying to ask, so I do it for her.

Maryann says, "She shot him to stop him from hurting her. Then she ran to the backyard and hid in the doghouse while he drove off."

"And then what?"

Valere sniffs. "He drove around the block."

Maryann says, "And died."

"Where did you shoot him?" Susie manages.

"Through both lungs and the heart." Valere is small and fine-featured. She wears her gray hair in a short cut and looks athletic in prison clothes. I like her. Susie likes her. Anyone would. She makes real eye contact; she means what she says. At this point in time, she's served eighteen years. "I'm lucky to have been here," she actually says. "It's given me time to look at myself and figure out what went wrong." She says when she gets out, she won't have much life left. "My people die early. I might make it to sixty-five." Her brother is suffering from kidney failure. She would like to get out in time to give him a kidney. Her eyes seem very large, very open wide.

It's hard to explain the intensity of these visits. They're like nothing else. Absorb and absorb and absorb. A new baby being brought to his mother. The mother in her prison garb reaching out for him. The waiting room, where we become like hostages held in another kind of cell. We can't leave. We can't get out. We wait and watch one another, and in little bits and pieces we have one, two, three more reasons for our hearts to break. Alone, it is almost more than I can bear. With Susie, I can enjoy seeing Maryann teased by her roommate when she doesn't speak up about her life. "Oh go on, Maryann, say it like it is. You're always so repressed!" Inmate Day Labor has been discontinued for a while and Maryann is working as a clerk in the mental ward. "It's peaceful," she says, although one woman hears voices that tell her to throw her lunch away and another woman believes she's being followed, so she sits in the office with Maryann and cries. The mental patients don't mix with the other prisoners. Life on the yard would be too hard for them, according to Maryann. "We have to get jobs. We have to take care of ourselves! There are rules. A lot of stress." Even in prison, there are prisons.

And what about the little cat, Nermal?

Maryann says he is locked up in Sheron's bathroom. It was supposed to be a temporary arrangement, but he has been kept in there for one reason or another. A window needs to be fixed. Or it's the heating or the air conditioning or the other cats. It begins to seem that Nermal, too, exchanged a large prison for a much smaller one. Night. Stars through a window. A lock on the door. Maryann doesn't want to talk about it. Finally, though, after a lot of thought, after months of deliberating, she and Valere have signed on as support providers in the puppy program, which means they have one or another dog with them for part of each day. "It's fabulous!" There will be letters and phone calls now full of news about the dogs, especially about a golden retriever named Jesse. "I think I'm in love," Maryann says. "And this time, he's worth it."

I tell her that I talk to her lawyer every few weeks. "He sounds good. Really smart. He basically thinks Stephen Hioki did everything he had to do. I mean, *had* to do. But he also says Hioki should have investigated William himself and not depended on the state to provide him with his information. That was crucial. It wouldn't have been hard to call California and learn about William's actual sentence. The other thing he says is that Hioki should have fought harder for a deal. For you. He should have gone to the prosecutors and said, 'Hey look, your boy took a lie-detector test and failed it and we'd like to give one to our client and make a deal for her.' " I decide not to tell her something else Mike Brennan had said, which was that Maryann had been in "a weird space" when she was arrested. "I don't know if this was still happening in Hawaii," he told me, "but in California she was, you know, in contact with William for quite a while after she was arrested, and she wouldn't co-operate in any deal against him."

I said to him, "It's called love."

I say to Maryann, "You never told me William failed a lie-detector test."

Maryann says, "I forgot."

"Plus, you kept protecting him."

"I know. He kept telling me I wouldn't go to prison if I did what he said. And if I didn't . . . there were threats. Even against my mom and dad. By the time I realized he didn't really have a bevy of followers taking his orders, it was too late to save myself and come clean."

"I've got a friend in Hawaii helping me do some research," I announce. "You know, I told you Charles Marsland, who was DA. He ran on a campaign of lock up the criminals and throw away the key because his nineteen-year-old son had been mur-dered on Waimanalo Beach back in 1975. The son was working at Infinity Disco in Waikiki and Marsland thought he'd over-heard something there that got him dragged off at four-thirty in the morning and shot in the head at the beach. For a long time I thought he believed Larry Hasker was killed by the same gang. But maybe he just needed a conviction in order to look good after his political campaign. Maybe Jan Futa was under orders to get a conviction or lose her job, and they didn't care who really killed Larry."

Valere's nodding, as if she's sure Maryann was framed, but Maryann shrugs and smiles at a woman who killed her mother and refuses to see her children or grandchildren, refuses to ask for parole because she doesn't want to be a burden to them. It was a mercy killing, but there you are. And there is the young mother who is cuddling the baby and then stands up when the COs announce a car in the parking lot with its lights on. "I'll go fix it!" she volunteers, and everyone, all of us in the visiting room, are able to laugh as one big happy-for-a-moment family. For a moment or longer, we are joined by this horrible joke. In fact, there is a good deal of joy all around, even as I see a woman circling the room with her husband, circling, circling, as if they are both trapped on one of those wheels that rodents have in their cages. Even if, outside, the rain pours down and only some of us will be leaving at eight o'clock.

Later, in the darkness of the airport parking lot, Susie closes her eyes for a minute. "I want to thank you for bringing me down here," she says. "I feel blessed by those two women."

I say I think I know what she means. "I'm starting to believe everyone needs a prisoner."

"What happened to William? What did he get out of it?"

"Mike Brennan says he didn't get much. If he'd been really smart, he'd have had an attorney for the Arauza case instead of trying to do it himself. He'd have had someone who could make a good deal for him. He'd already testified in other cases and they owed him big-time. But Brennan says William was still stupid back then. Meaning maybe he's not anymore. Anyway, he got nothing for all his testimonies except being moved out of California and having some tattoos removed. The tattoos made him look like he was in the Paramount gang, which he never was. Paramount is where he's from, and Brennan says these guys go into prison and they get tattoos to make them look like they're protected. Then they get moved to another prison, where that's the wrong gang. So that's what he got for betraying the girl he married. He got his tattoos taken off."

Susie says tiredly, "And so forth." Having lived in California all her life, this is a piece of it she's never seen. Then she asks, "Is Brennan any good?"

"He filed a writ of habeas corpus the same week I first wrote to her. I thought something would have happened by now. It's maddening. And yes, I believe in him." I had told Mike Brennan that I'd been on Maryann's jury, that I'd been kicked off, that I would like to help, and he'd said I was welcome to call. It was hard for him to communicate with Maryann, since the phone system at his office didn't accept collect calls and he could not call her at the prison. The thing I could do was to help them stay in touch with each other.

"You got kicked off that jury," Susie says, "for the same reason Jan Futa had to put a muzzle on. They knew you were a not-guilty vote. They knew it from the first day. Maryann was framed, wasn't she?"

A few days later. I tell Maryann on the phone how tired we were. How we sat in the airport parking lot trying to remember all the things we'd talked about and how we had finally just climbed out of the car and onto the plane. Maryann laughs. "Oh, it's the same thing in here. We're always completely wiped out after a visiting day. You want to go straight to bed and put your head under the pillow." She says, "But don't ever think it doesn't mean a lot to us. Did I ever tell you about the time Doug, my biological dad, and his wife came to see me for a seventy-two-hour visit? They brought one of their kids, Shawn, and it was great, really, but I was so nervous going into it. I'd met them all before, but seventy-two hours is a long time. And do you know what?" She sounds almost childlike as the words tumble out. "I had gone through so much with Mom, and finally she'd given me the adoption papers, and then when I set up the visit, I was worried about telling them. But Mom said, 'Well, maybe we'll come on down there,' which was crazy, but the visit with Doug and Pat and Shawn was Monday through Wednesday, and Thursday was a normal visiting day back then. And my parents did come, and it was wonderful because the others stayed. Maybe one of the best days of my life. Can you imagine how extremely wrung out I was afterward? They were all here together and we spent hours like that just laughing and thanking each other. Even in a place like this you can have good memories." She adds that Doug has since had a stroke and can no longer visit or speak on the phone.

48

Then I called Joe Leach. It was easy enough to find him on the Internet. He was living in California, not too many miles from Maryann. I said I had been on the jury in the Maryann Acker murder trial, and for a minute he didn't know what I was talking about. Then he said, "Oh, it was so long ago." He said he'd seen an article in the *Los Angeles Times* a few years ago but that he didn't really think about it anymore. The article was the one about L.A. County's jailhouse informant scandal in which William was featured prominently.

"She's still in prison," I said.

And he said, "Well, I hope so."

It wasn't what I expected after reading his testimony. On the stand, he had said, "I couldn't tell what she was feeling inside," and I had taken that for a sign that he realized she might have been acting under duress, might have been scared, might have been stupid or passive. On the stand, he'd portrayed William as wild and unpredictable and frightening. I'd assumed that the prosecutor had not asked further questions because she did not want to expose his doubts, and I'd assumed that Hioki was not doing a good job of cross-examining.

It's possible that the years have hardened Joe Leach.

It's possible that I don't want to know what he would have said if they'd let him say it. His captors had taken his camera and pawned it. But when the L.A. police confiscated William's small bag, it had a roll of film inside with twenty-four photographs taken with Maryann's Christmas Instamatic. What were they? I can only guess. A child playing with an inflatable tube on a beach. A row of palm trees reaching like toothpicks for the sky. A slim girl wearing a blue bikini, holding her hands in front of her face as if to ward off the painfulness of a flash. "Where are the photographs?" I ask Maryann, and she says she has no idea. "They were confiscated." I imagine a picture of William. He's standing in the Western store at Ala Moana, trying on a hat. It's a Stetson, very dark, and he's smiling under it. He's wearing jeans and a cream-colored button-down shirt. His hair, under the hat, is brown and slightly wavy. He has sideburns, black shoes, and the look of a desert creature caught in strong headlights. The rest of the pictures? There are three of them, all blurry, of a mongoose standing up on his hind feet. "Oh look, he's posing for us," Maryann had chirped on the night they had stayed in a cave at the bay.

William must have had good memories of this place where he'd come with his other wife and her child, where he'd felt normal for two or three hours as he put on a mask and went out in the ocean to look at the fish. He didn't know how to swim, but he managed to move around in the water, holding on to the reef. You have to be raised to swim, and he was the farthest thing from raised like that. What he had was smarts. What he had was his shitty life, but he'd survived, and now he was back here where he'd dreamed about with a new wife and things were working out, and when they closed up the park, maybe they'd just stick around, since there was no reason to leave.

Except that Joe Leach is sitting in the Garden Bar at the Hilton Hawaiian Village. Maybe Larry Hasker is there, too. The Garden Bar is a hangout, a meeting place, and Larry and Joe both go there often. At the Garden Bar, tourists mingle with locals, which produces a pleasant energy. By the time William meets up with Larry a few nights after the long night at Hanauma Bay, Larry's looking for someone called "Red." "See a guy with a red beard come through here?" he asks William. But William doesn't bite. He's sitting alone on a bench on the open lanai outside the bar.

Larry enters the bar. It's after ten and Red's late, or maybe Red doesn't exist. Maybe it is all a way to catch William. He notices a tall blonde. Pretty girl! Offers her a drink. She walks to a table as if she knows where she's going. Soft hair. Says her name is Carole. "You from around here?" he asks.

"Not really." She has a slow kind of voice.

So he guesses. "New Mexico. Arizona. I have a good ear."

She covers her mouth as if where she comes from is a secret. Then she says, "I'm thinking you're local, though." Because she likes him; he's nice. And William won't bother with this guy if he's from here.

The drinks arrive. Hers is a margarita.

"Want to dance?" Larry asks.

But she sees William giving her the signal. "Can you wait for me just a sec? My brother. He's keeping an eye on me."

Outside, William says, "What's the deal?"

"He's from here." Assuming she has saved Larry Hasker from the kind of ride William had forced on Joe Leach, Maryann returns to the table.

A minute later, William sits down with them. Hasker and Maryann are smoking. The music is loud. William is snapping his fingers. Hasker feels Maryann's nearness, smells the pleasantness of her hair. William says, "We're going to a disco, Carole. Remember? Meet a guy about a music deal." So it's good. He wants to leave. Hasker is safe.

Then. "You're in music. I figured." Hasker asks what disco they're going to and says maybe he'll meet up with them later.

First, there was the nice returned missionary and then there was William. He just moved in. He advanced on Maryann's heart and mind and house and they started to drink and have sex, and he was always talking too fast; it all happened too fast; his hands and mouth were all over her. He was living in the place she kept so clean, sleeping on her water bed, using her comb and toothbrush. He made her look at him. Listen to the music he liked. Drink beer. Iron a crease in his jeans. He was almost thirty. She'd been buried in her stupid, sheltered life, but he needed her. He got fired for smoking in the back of the warehouse, but they were getting married. He got a job pumping gas. He got fired again. In bed, he was too fast, but it was understandable, and they did it everyplace—on the floor in bed in the car. They drank. They called her parents. He managed it. She was tired from getting up and he'd bother her. He'd call her at work. He'd say, "Get me some money. I'll meet you outside." He'd say, "Get me some money. I'm taking your car." He'd say, "Get me some money. I'm leaving you." Her parents should have locked her up. He'd tell her to cash a check and have money ready when he came by in her car. She couldn't concentrate. So she quit her job and got another one at a little restaurant in the mall, but he'd stand outside and watch, and when he was watching, she'd forget who she was. It's hard to believe how she disappeared, but she'd known him a month, and they were husband and wife. She had a duty, and in Hawaii, when they got off the plane, didn't he know where he was? He called himself "Spirit," and she was supposed to carry his knife, which was like a seal, like something more meaningful than the wedding, because he thought God did not exist, and maybe He didn't, but maybe He did, and when he slid up against her those first few days, it didn't matter anymore.

At 2:00 a.m., it's deserted out at Hanauma Bay. The moon is there behind clouds and the stars are reflected in dark, living water. A picture can be made of the sleeping fish, the coral reef, everything alive but asleep, and William tells Larry to get out of the car. There is the sound of water beating against land. Think of it. You could tease God and fool your parents and go home afterward, but this was different. To know you were living your life.

Honolulu

49

October 2005.

I had thought of the end of this story as an afternoon on the old courthouse steps, Maryann's long blue muumuu starched by the trade winds as she stands looking out at the mountains, finally free. Mike Brennan is talking to the intern he's brought along from California. The two of them are tall and serious amid the various locals who mingle around the courthouse, many of whom are about to make their own pleas. Yes, Maryann is a dream we have dreamed, but instead of coming out of the old courthouse with victory dripping off us like earned perspiration, we are going into a new circuit court building, wondering if we have identified each other accurately.

Mike Brennan looks assured, uncompromising, and as smart as I want him to be. Maryann has told me she feels good in his presence, and I do, too, although, when I speak to him in the hallway, when I slide in behind him as he steps into the courtroom, I have to pretend that I'm filling a necessary place, bearing witness because Maryann isn't here.

We've entered a paneled room without windows. There is the echo of thunder. The local lawyer is saying, "Thunder? It just doesn't happen here. I can't remember when . . ." And I think, Not since March 1982. There was thunder then, too.

Twenty-three years. Even without windows, I can feel the courtroom darken as the other team unpacks boxes and boxes of files. Someone named Fudo is going to represent Jan Futa and Colleen Hirai, who was apparently dismissed as the first prosecutor in Maryann's trial.

While Fudo and his assistant arrange papers on their table, another man comes in: tall, good-looking, salt-and-peppery Japanese. He has a familiar jutting chin and high cheekbones, a spoon with sharp edges. This must be Stephen Hioki, since he offers his help to Mike Brennan and then takes his leave.

Next, Judge Town enters and we are commanded to rise. I am the only spectator in the room. No reporter. No one else at all. Apparently no one but the lawyers and a long-ago juror cares about Maryann's fate. The bailiff asks us to be seated. Judge Town wishes us a good morning. He is a small man with a pink face. His voice is slightly falsetto.

Brennan is an outsider here—a real haole—and he looks distinctly out of place. When he stands, he seems to loom over his adversaries at the next table, and the looming is more than physical. He says that he is going to establish three things: first, that in 1982, the state of Hawaii failed to provide Maryann's defense attorney with vital information about William's sentence in California; second, that it failed to disclose his jailhouse activities as an informant; and third, that it allowed William to perjure himself. Knowingly. Important parts of William's testimony were lies, Brennan reminds Judge Town, and the prosecutors knew that. Hioki was given an FBI rap sheet on William that was inaccurate. The reason this matters is that Hioki might have argued his case differently if he had known William's actual sentence. Judge Au might have made his decisions differently and the jury might have weighed William's testimony differently. If everyone had understood that William had the possibility of parole, they would have understood that he had something to gain by testifying against his wife. Further, if they had known that he had been used by other prosecutors to give false testimony, his words on the stand would have been discredited.

The first witness Brennan calls to the stand is Colleen Hirai, who insists that she played no part in the case and that, as far as her dismissal is concerned, she remembers nothing. I hear the local defense attorney who is assisting Brennan suggest in a loud whisper that Hirai was dismissed because she questioned the ethics or legality of what her boss, Charles Marsland, was willing to do to convict Maryann.

Doesn't matter. They'll put her away.

"They kicked her off the case," he tells Brennan with a hiss.

Brennan gives up on her fairly quickly and calls Jan Futa, the woman who actually prosecuted Maryann in 1982 and who has been fighting off this inquisition for five years. For the last half hour, she has stood in the hall conferring with her lawyers, her black shoe furiously tapping at the polished floor. Wearing a good suit and a grim face, she is, like all of us, twenty-three years older. The spark is gone. On the stand, she explains in a surly voice that she is a lawyer in private practice, and, yes, in 1982 she was a prosecutor. But it was a long time ago, she says, eerily echoing Maryann's words during the murder trial. When Brennan asks if she remembers that trial, she stares at him. "It was a long time ago," she says again, although I remember her concluding argument very well. "Quite conveniently there are many things [Maryann Acker] doesn't remember," she had told the jury, "because it's hard to fabricate things if there is no basis of truth." Now, to every question, her answer is more or less the same. "I don't remember," or "It was a long time ago," or "I don't recall."

"If I showed you these documents, would they refresh your memory?" Brennan asks. He hands over the letter Maryann had told me about, the one sent from California to the prosecutor's office early in 1982. It explains William's sentence, including the possibility of his parole. "Wouldn't this indicate that you were aware of the sentence and therefore knew that Acker had perjured himself?" The letter was received and stamped by Jan Futa.

"Hmm." Leaning over, frowning. "Well, I can't say whether these are originals. . . ." Futa has been given several months to review the documents. The hearing has been repeatedly delayed. What difference do any of us make in the world? What matters? Two young people were wicked and indifferent and cruel. They harmed and killed. And there is no undoing such things; there is only to recognize and then to reclaim whatever can be saved.

Brennan gives Judge Town the background facts. Maryann's California case was heard by a Mormon judge who was under investigation for making obscene phone calls and needed a conviction for his own reasons. Her lawyer for that trial was assigned to her. He was a prosecutor. He had never defended anyone before. There was no jury in that trial—the judge made Maryann agree to that—and she was not called to the stand to testify. William was still telling her he would "take the fall" and get her clear. He had taken that mysterious bus ride to Yuma after she'd been arrested. He had gone to her father. So, following William's instructions, she had insisted that she was driving Arauza's car only because her husband had given it to her. And the judge, who admitted that there was no evidence that she had touched the gun, convicted her for being present when Arauza was killed. The conviction of felony murder was Maryann's, not William's. But that is only the beginning of what the jury in Hawaii was not told.

Judge Town looks worried. "This is a big deal," he says sternly to the lawyers. He adds that if the state is required to remedy the situation, it may decide to reduce Maryann's sentence.

But Brennan draws himself up and insists that they must overturn Maryann's conviction. Vacate it. Nothing less will do.

Silence.

Then Fudo, who has the face of a predator, says Hioki obviously knew William's sentence. He had to have known. Why not call him to refute or support?

Judge Town seems relieved. "I would have assumed," he says to Brennan crossly, "that you'd have done that!"

But Brennan had been told that the state was going to subpoena Hioki. "It was made clear," he answers testily.

"You will get him in here tomorrow morning," the judge snaps back. "Or I'll do it myself."

The legal wrangling went on all day. We broke for lunch and I looked after Mike Brennan and his intern but went my own way. Once outside, in the hallway, I felt shy and covert although in the courtroom, it was frustrating not to be able to interrupt when Fudo insisted that William's sentence would not have mattered to the jury. Why bother the state of Hawaii about something that would not have made any difference? he demanded. Why bother the state of Hawaii with a proceeding that is trying to exonerate someone who was, at the very least, an accomplice to an extremely vicious murder? But Fudo did not use that argument more than once, which was interesting. The state, in 1982, had prosecuted Maryann as the shooter. In spite of Judge Au's improper instructions to the jury, when he declared that an accomplice is as guilty of murder as a shooter is, it would not do to point out her role as accomplice now. It would look like the state had prosecuted and convicted the wrong person, which is, of course, what they had done. "And why dredge up old bits and pieces of evidence that were fully examined to everyone's satisfaction twenty-some years ago?"

Fudo asked peevishly. After all, he implied, if nothing else, Maryann went along with this loser. Too bad she's spending her sorry life in prison, but that's what happens when you pick someone up in a bar and leave him dead next to the highway.

Maybe. But doesn't it matter whether or not she had a fair trial? Doesn't it matter that William was never charged with the murder, that he was the prime witness for the prosecution in spite of his history? Doesn't it matter that her lawyer never knew that William might have exchanged false testimony for an earlier parole? Doesn't truth, in its minutest particular, matter?

Or do we allow this conspiracy of silence?

In one of my father's letters—the ones he wrote to my mother during he war—he describes the pleasure he takes in setting things right. "My darling," he wrote on September 21, 1944, "it has really been a day so far and promises to continue in the same manner until far into the night even as it did last night. The only thing I haven't had to do is the one thing I wanted to do—read more letters from you. None came but I really can't complain after yesterday. Of course my principal concern has been the court-martial cases which begin tomorrow. They involve two lads who are accused, unjustly I hope, of theft and other sins against the dignity of the navy. The cases really involve a number of interesting features, both of fact and law (as all of my cases always do I am afraid). The situation arouses my crusading instincts and you are indeed fortunate to be several thousand miles away so you don't have to listen to me until far into the night. If it sounds good to you then you are really lonesome because you know how tiresome I am when on a crusade. But you really have no idea how the whole situation has pepped me up."

As my mother had promised, the letters are full of holes, carefully snipped, but the words left untouched were loving, personal, and passionate. They are written by a father I never knew, although his defense of enlisted men against the "powers that be" were the only war stories he brought home. "To my inward delight I was able deferentially to point out that the precept convening the court was fatally defective," he wrote on February 23, 1944.

Oh, how satisfying that must have been.

I had reconnected with Maryann out of guilt, but there was more to it now and perhaps the crusade had pepped me up. The next morning I was at the courthouse in time to buy a cup of coffee in the shop just off the lobby.

The coffee was in a pot on a hot plate and the woman who took my coins was blind, which seemed at that moment to be significant. Was she the same woman who had taken my coins twenty-three years ago? Blind. Justice. Upstairs, I saw Stephen Hioki, and when I introduced myself, he said, "On the jury? Still following the case?" Perhaps he has battled enough windmills. "I don't remember a whole lot about that trial," he said, "but I remember my moments with Maryann. I don't know what it was, but she was different than any other client I ever had."

Court was called into session. I was making notes in the old yellow notebook—the smooth yellow surface, the red spine. It was precisely when I realized that I would take it back to Hawaii that I knew I had come on this long journey with Maryann in order to finish the things left undone in my own life. There were blank pages at the back of the book. Bare lines. "The transcripts seem to indicate that I was under the impression," Hioki was saying, "that Mr. Acker had life without parole. It seems I was interested in impeaching him because he couldn't have been convicted of felony murder if he was sentenced to life without parole. I was sure he must have been convicted of first degree because I had researched the law and that sentence would not have applied to the lesser crime." I could see Hioki as a young man, ardent in his green pants and brown jacket. He thought William was the shooter in California, but he had made one glaring mistake. I had read the old newspaper articles before I flew to Hawaii for this hearing, and on March 24, 1982, a reporter for the *Star Bulletin,* Hawaii's evening paper, had reported that William Acker did, in fact, have the possibility of parole. Did the defense lawyer not read newspapers? Could he not have called California to check on William's sentence as that reporter must have done? An error of omission. An error of enormous consequence. "I may have slowed down a little these days, Your Honor," Hioki noted, looking up at the judge, "but in those days I was relentless. I was passionate about holding the state to its burden of proof. I used up my fees before even coming to trial. There were only three witnesses to the murder and one was dead. I had to do everything in my power to show that Mr. Acker was not credible. I tried to prove his untruthfulness, to show that his version of the murder was false, that Mr. Hasker's shirt wasn't torn, that there were two bullets fired, not three. We had ballistics supporting our facts. Larry Hasker was shot from the back to the front at a fifteen-degree angle. But Mr. Acker said Maryann was facing him and fired three shots. I would have been glad to have a motive for his blaming Maryann. To know that he had the possibility of parole, or to know that he was a jailhouse informant, would have helped my case!"

No wonder William had sat in the witness stand with a smirk on his face. He had not expected it to be so easy. Even now, his lethal spirit stalked the little courtroom so that the cross fire went on for two more hours, until Fudo, who was in a hurry to pick up his daughter at school, said it boiled down to two different counsels having different strategies. Not so, Brennan said, making a final, stunning argument in Maryann's defense. "Two different strategies?" He sounded astonished. "The fact is," he said in a gravelly voice, "that there is no evidence in the record that says Hioki did *anything* for strategic reasons. This is not about Mr. Hioki's strategy. This is about the state's obligation. They were there to do justice, to get the right person convicted. And they failed to do that. They failed because they used the testimony of a witness who repeatedly perjured himself and who did so with their knowledge. They failed because they used the testimony of a witness who repeatedly sold himself to prosecutors. They had the obligation to tell defense that their prime witness was a known informant, and that he had turned state's evidence because he had been sentenced to life with the possibility of parole in California and was hoping to reduce his ultimate sentence."

Judge Town had worked with Fudo and Hioki and Jan Futa many times over the years. As he put it, "I've had each of you in my courtroom; we know each other well." It was not pleasant to contemplate wrongdoing on the part of any of these colleagues. There were reputations at stake, including his own.

50

spent the next day retracing Maryann's steps. The Makiki Arms was gone now, but there were still similar two-story buildings in the old neighborhood. I had spent a summer in one of them when I visited my brother and his first wife in 1958. Their baby, my nephew, was six months old, and I used to push him up and down the sidewalks in his stroller, feeling pleased with my newfound grown-up self. Now it was a shock to find the old place, and I wondered why I had never looked for it in all the years I'd lived in Hawaii. The cinder-block building was behind a big Victorian house and well off the street, so maybe I had driven down Thurston and assumed that it had disappeared. Maybe I had not wanted to disrupt my happy memories. How enchanted life in that place had seemed, lying on the little *punee* in the living room, listening to the rattling of palm trees and the hooting of ships. Listening to LP records on Sunday mornings: *Pictures at an Exhibiton* with bacon and scrambled eggs. These days, a rough driveway slopes down to the apartments and there are various broken-down cars parked on what once was grass. The backyard, which looked so magnificently down on the harbor, has been peeled away and there is a tall building jutting up from what is now a huge hole in the earth. I used to hang diapers on the line back there after we did the wash. I used to imagine myself grown-up and married. I would come back to the islands, eat Japanese food. I would be more like my brother and less like myself. My brother, the taker of risks.

Only a block from my brother's apartment, Maryann and William lived, very briefly, during what was supposed to be their honeymoon. A balcony ran across the front of that building and underneath, on ground level, was the laundry room with its pay phone and the washing machine where William hid the gun. In front was the parking lot, where he put Larry Hasker's car when he took him upstairs. A little later— not much later—William and Larry and Maryann came back down. Larry's hands were tied behind his back and his shirt was riding his shoulders. Larry was saying, "Ah come on, man, this can't be real."

William told Larry that it was.

From Thurston and the nonexistent Makiki Arms, I drove to the building where Larry Hasker had once lived with his sister, Kimberly. It still looms in an ugly way over the main commercial corner near the university, and I had a beer in Puck's Alley, where I used to go on long, warm afternoons. Was this Maryann's past or mine?

Before I moved to Canada in 1982, I drove around the island to say good-bye. It was like drowning—passing my best friend's house, where she lived all alone, where she was raped, where her dog was killed, where the screen porch was something she built by and for herself. Just a shack, now that I look at it, but a room of her own. And farther on, to the place where both my parents sat one day, Mother saying, "Let's have our lunch here." My father had parked the car and we had pretended happiness. It was the last time I would see him alive.

Up by Haleiwa, the preschool I visited when I worked in child care. The lukewarm welcome and the hot lunch. I had an office on the second floor of a Congregational church on the outskirts of Kailua. The agency I had created provided federally funded child care to low-income families, some of them local and some remnants of families like mine who had fled the mainland during the 1960s. The white women were single mothers like me, divorced, living far from home. The local families were poor but intact.

My office window overlooked the Kawanui Marsh, which had once been part of the sea. On its edge sat the remains of the ancient *heiau* called Ulupo—a great level platform of stones, very potent, very carefully placed. At night, I went back to my children and stared into the darkness of the garden, trying to understand the mysteries of the island, the bloodlines, the antagonism against people who come from outside. Someday, I told myself, I'll come back to Hawaii and drive along any street, any beach road and remember my life. I'll be able to say, here's X's house or Y's. The Buddhist temple Michael and I visited that day we knew everything. The cove where we swam. And the house of the former prosecutor. The one who said, "They'll put her away."

Instead, it was another trail entirely that I was following. I drove to the Hilton, where William and Maryann met Larry Hasker and Joe Leach. The Garden Bar is gone now, like so much else, but I went out and watched three or four children scraping around in the sand that covered the spot where Maryann had danced with Joe after she ordered her drink.

Then I had a great desire to see my old house, to see what had become of it and how I would feel standing in the shade of the front-yard tree. It was a fig, with big stiff leaves. "Ours was a 3 bedroom, 2 bath house, no garage, but a covered carport," Maryann had finally written, describing her childhood home and my own Hawaii house at the same time. "The kitchen, narrow and long, was at the front, with a window facing the street above the sink." I had waited five years for that description, but everything that matters was left out—whatever it was that happened within those walls, and the child, and the reason her need to be needed was so great.

In truth, the fig tree is gone and it was hard to imagine us there: my girls with long hair and long legs running up the street as if everything—the dolls and stuffed animals, the dog, the friends, and the grandmother—would not disappear.

On the way to Kailua, I had gone the long way out of Waikiki. The day was beautifully clear, with the hills shouting their greens on the left side of the highway and the ocean swirling on the right. There is the expensive suburb of Black Point and then Kahala, and after that I could smell the old, dry dustiness of the soil as I drove beyond houses and gardens and along the barren expanse of rocky beach that stretches to Koko Head, that startling crater that rises up on one side of Hanauma Bay. There is a legend that involves a beautiful girl who is fought over by two young men. Fearing the rivals will harm each other, she turns herself into this crater, sacrificing her life while her father stretches out to protect her, forming the arms of Hanauma Bay. I thought of Larry and William. And Maryann. Bert Bray reaching out to his child. The night before, I'd dreamed about my mother sitting at the table I was trying to set. I was doing my best, but her pretty dishes, the family heirlooms, kept shattering in my hands.

I drove past Koko Head. In the distance, as I curled in and out of the curves of the road, I caught glimpses of the windward side—Makapu'u, Lanikai, and the twin islands we once knew like friends. Then I pulled off the road, preparing myself for the sadness I'd feel at the murder site. How eerie and fugitive I felt, as if I should mark the spot with one of those Mexican crosses, or leave a sacred stone wrapped in a fresh ti leaf.

I got out of the car as Larry and Joe had done and looked down.

It is different now. There are hundreds of people on the sand. There is a building, a ticket booth. There is an entrance fee, an educational video. How to not damage the coral. How to protect the fish.

Hard to imagine murder here.

Except that up near the highway, there is still the rutted road and those brambly kiawe trees. There is still a drop that hasn't been smoothed and the spirits that stick to this place, and I could imagine Maryann and her brand-new husband spending the night in one of the hillside caves. In the morning, waking up, feeling the sunrise slippery and fast, did they swim? Did they spend the next hours with the tourists looking at fish, or did they climb back up to the highway and wait for the bus to take them back to a day of planning and arguing? In her letters and conversations, Maryann never says what they did. What she says is, "If you like who you are now, you have to accept your past."

At the hearing, when Mike Brennan described the murder of Cesario Arauza to Judge Town, he said it was done "execution-style." He said Arauza's arms were crossed over his chest, he was lying on his back, and he had been shot in the head. "Do you think an eighteen-year-old girl is physically capable of that?" The conversation took place during a recess, and I was listening, sitting on the sidelines with my notebook, more or less out of sight. Hearing Brennan's words, I felt real surprise. He wasn't working to overturn Maryann's conviction because it was theoretically possible or because he had students who needed the work. Mike Brennan believed in Maryann's innocence.

There was dismay, too, which was another surprise. Because if Maryann isn't guilty, my own guilt is worse.

Those lost five minutes that cost her life.

Leaving Honolulu, we took off to windward, as usual, flying over Pearl Harbor and the Aloha Tower, and then I could see the palace, white in the sunlight, as if that little monarchy had ever stood a chance. I've watched the coastline of O'ahu diminish so many times, ever farther and farther away, that from above it looks like the back of my hand, as familiar to me as fingers, knuckles, veins, and wrist. There is the sky and the light and the swallowing sea and the beautiful circular bay. Who, in such a severe and archaic place, could kidnap and rob and kill? Squinting, I could almost see the events taking place. Nineteen seventy-eight. The risen moon, the tiny tableau. Looking down at the surf, where children are still and forever playing, I thought of the moray eel I'd met in that same reef long ago. My brother must have been somewhere ahead, not far away, urging me on, but he was not near enough to save me from the sight of the open mouth and murderous teeth. Years of remembering, and still there is no way of knowing how such a creature does what he does or sees what he sees of the world.

51

Three months later, Judge Town overturned Maryann's 1982 conviction. Again, local papers painted her as the villain. TWO-TIME KILLER GRANTED A NEW TRIAL read a headline in the *Advertiser.*

"He did it! He did it!" I shouted into the phone, because Maryann could not get through to Mike Brennan. I could hear her initial scream of excitement. I could hear her shouting to her friends and to Jesse, the dog. Then Maryann got quiet. "I'll be here awhile yet," she said. "The state will appeal. Mike will offer them a deal and they won't take it. So there will have to be another trial. The state supreme court this time. It could take years. And you know, it's still California that decides my fate, even if Hawaii lets me go."

In 1978, Maryann was given what is known as an indeterminate sentence—seven years to life—for being present during the Arauza murder. In the past, an inmate usually served six to ten years with this sentence, but the California parole board is appointed by the governor, and the last two or three have changed the rules. There are twenty-five women at CIW who have been approved for parole but have never been released. There are a great many more who have never been approved. Maryann Acker is one of those.

So. We wait, clock face uncracked.

When Sheron, the Mormon visitor, dies, I am the only one left on the outside. Then Maryann receives a letter from her foster sister, Pauline. When she tells me that Pauline lives on the Navajo reservation in Arizona and that she has only a cell phone that Maryann can't call, I carry my own phone into my Toronto garden, and dial the number Maryann has given me. The Mormons believe that Native Americans, whom they call "Lamanites," are descended from one of the lost tribes of Israel and that, although they have "dwindled in disbelief," they will blossom as the rose once they return to the fold and become "a white and delightsome people." Because of this prophecy, the Mormons had swept onto the Navajo reservation when Pauline was five or six years old, admonishing parents to give up their children. Post haste.

Pauline's mother had complied.

Pauline told me that one night, without explanation, she was packed onto a bus and sent into the darkness on the long trip down to Phoenix. "I knew two words of English," she told me. "*No* and *yes*." She was frightened and alone and, in the middle of the night, the children were taken off the bus, hosed down, and deloused in a Phoenix ward house. There, Pauline was assigned to her foster parents, Gladys and Bert Bray. She followed Gladys and Bert, Penne and Maryann out to a car. How strange it must have seemed. "I remember riding in the backseat and then getting out when they parked in a driveway. I remember Maryann took my hand and led me across the yard.

She wanted to show me off to all her neighbors. She was so excited that I was there. 'This is my new sister' is what she was saying, but I couldn't understand a word. All the way there, sitting in the backseat, I didn't know what any of them were saying. Now Maryann was holding my hand real sweetly, but I was so tired, I could hardly walk. Did I want to go with her? I said one of my two words. I said yes."

Pauline's memories uncoiled while I sat in my garden holding the phone. At last I was hearing the details of Maryann's childhood. "The family was really involved with church. I didn't like it, but I had to go. I could never get sick on Sunday. The first Sunday of the month, we fasted until evening. And every Sunday morning, we went to church for several hours. Maryann was always giving her testimony up front and our mom was always asking me if I was ready. I always said no. On Sunday evenings we went back to church. The grown-ups would talk. It wasn't Scripture. I don't remember anyone talking about the Bible, only about the Book of Mormon."

The next time Maryann called, I told her everything. She said she didn't remember her Sunday testimonies. She didn't remember Pauline speaking Navajo. She didn't remember taking her around to the neighbors. Maybe she blanked out the horrible murders and then everything else went the same way. If she could talk to Pauline, maybe it would all come back. But if she doesn't want to remember? If it's easier to live in the present? I miss my family because a lot of my past died with them, and my memories are not reliable. I can barely remember dancing with my father, it seems so unlikely now. His ease and confidence on the dance floor, his passion for ideas, for good food, for beautiful women, for justice, for life. I do remember wanting to keep up with him. Wanting to take my feet off the ground so that he would bear my weight. "Spell *precipitous*," my father ordered. And I finally did.

In October 2006, I met Pauline at the airport near Corona. We had decided to celebrate Maryann's forty-seventh birthday with a visit to the prison. We had trouble finding each other. We were both nervous. This visit meant a night of getting acquainted over dinner, a short sleep, and then an early venture into the cow pastures, which are rapidly being converted to housing developments. Any traces of landscape I might have recognized had disappeared over the last six months. Our little plug-in GPS system would not accept the prison address, so we were more or less on our own and, as usual, I got lost. Pauline was composed. "I don't think this GPS thing is working."

"No."

"I'm just going to drive to where I remember it was. Over there." She pointed at the distant hills.

"You visited once, for an hour, twenty years ago."

"Right."

"And you remember those hills."

"Of course."

As Pauline drove, she told me she had never understood the sequence of events in Maryann's life. "Our mom told me Maryann was away at school. For years, they didn't tell me the truth, and for a while I was living out here in California, real close to the prison. I could have been visiting."

"Why didn't they tell you?"

"Denial. The church. Shame. Finally, they showed me some articles when I went to see them. They said Maryann's husband hypnotized her and got her in trouble." She studied the street signs. Chino-Corona, the road to the prison, was closed. Pauline shook her head and turned off another way. "I think Maryann just got tired of the strict rules. There were so many. Things you couldn't eat or drink. Coke. Bacon. I don't remember all of them. Penne got in trouble because she wanted to go with some friends on a picnic on Sunday. Penne loved to party. Penne had a vehicle. We weren't allowed in her room, but it was full of makeup and records and hair things, and we used to sneak in and try on her things and she'd find out and tell her mom. I wasn't ever jealous of Maryann; she was my sister—

more than my own sisters. The oldest one never liked me and the younger one is so much younger, but Maryann was mine. I didn't think about whose toys or who had more clothes. I never thought of it. She got invited to more birthday parties, but she'd ask them to invite me, and they would. I understand her wanting to do something different," she said again. "Her family being really strict. But she was always good. I was the one who got into trouble, and she always took the blame for me."

I said, "Well, later on she took it for William."

Once we found the prison, the wait was not long, and I enjoyed sitting out on the curb, looking at the horrible fence and listening to Pauline's stories about her childhood. She had only kind words for Bert and Gladys, but many bitter memories of Penne. "I went back to the house after Mom's funeral and she kept me apart from her family."

When the locked door to the visiting room was clicked open, I stood back and watched Pauline and Maryann rush into each other's arms. The tears and caresses caused everyone, even the guards, to look away for a moment. It was early morning and we found seats in the sunshine outside. Then, for the next three hours, I listened. I had meant to ask questions, but Maryann was enjoying herself and what, finally, would be the point? The reminiscences they shared were not consequential. Nothing important was revealed. Mom's cooking. Dad's work hours. Penne's boyfriends. The family cockapoo. I listened. But Maryann smiled and smiled. Yes. Yes. At eleven o'clock, Dexter, the golden retriever Maryann is training, was brought to a window in the back corner of the room so that we could admire him. When he saw Maryann, he leaped against the thick glass, trying to make contact with her. Then Valere arrived and Pauline became quiet—Pauline, the childhood roommate. Valere, the grown-up cell mate. Maryann told us about Cadet, one of the dogs the inmates had trained who was coming back for a visit with his new mistress, a nine-year-old girl named Kayla, who was born without legs. "Cadet does everything for her. She only has one arm that doesn't bend, but she's such a trouper. She even skis. Her folks made her a kind of bucket, and Cadet grabs hold of her hood and runs along behind." Over popcorn and tacos, we heard plenty of dog stories. The CIW inmates have become professional trainers. They keep the dogs with them in their cells, grow attached, train them to turn on lights and signal seizures and other astonishing things. Then the dogs graduate and leave.

It was a few days before Maryann's forty-seventh birthday and we were trying to celebrate. Penne's husband had sold the Phoenix house and disappeared with the money. There was no word from the Hawaii Supreme Court—no decision on the state's appeal. I lost nine dollars in the vending machines but we managed to purchase a piece of cheesecake for Maryann and she managed to chew. While we cheered her on, Valere told Pauline about the woman they all called "Band-Aid" because she used to pull her cheeks tight with Band-Aids or Scotch tape in order to look younger. "Even when she was dying of cancer," Valere said, chuckling, "she lay in her bed with her face taped up tight."

"Seems like there's always another cancer story."

"Lots of it in here. Even with the staff. The place is toxic."

"You guys should do a study. Find out statistics about the population here."

"Like abuse?" Valere said. "Most of the women here were abused. As kids. And here's something. A whole lot of these women were adopted. That's interesting."

At three o'clock, Maryann and Pauline clung to each other for several minutes while the guard looked away. "She didn't rush us," Maryann said later on the phone. "I couldn't believe it. That's never happened before. It meant so much to me to see Pauline. You've given me back my childhood."

I said, "You've given me back my life."

We had been the last visitors to leave except for a little girl, holding on to her mother, crying. "Go with Grandma," her mother said softly. "Go on now. I'll see you soon." But the little girl kept sobbing. She sobbed all the way out to the parking lot while her grandmother kept a protective arm around her little shoulders, and I felt that I wouldn't make it to the car. Nausea. Misery. I wanted it all to be over.

52

This year, I walk to the bank of the river, moving down the rocks like an animal because I know this patch of earth in my muscles by now. The ground between the house and the river is covered by pine needles, so it's slippery, and I move under the enormous trees, which are black as silhouettes.

In late August, the water is a shock. Three minutes, Michael promises. When I plunge then, it is for his smile. Today I notice the wavering lines of light on the trunk of a tree, alternating ribbons of dark and light. Michael is several yards ahead of me, but I shout, "What makes it do that?" I see, now, that trees all around me are doing this—reflecting light. Their trunks and branches appear to be decomposing, and I'm astonished and dismayed that every morning I've stayed in bed drinking coffee while all this has been going on.

Across from us are the rapids, which pour and pour until they freeze in the winter and then break up and pour again.

Around us, in a great circle, are the riverbanks, except where the channel of the smaller branch of the river cuts in quietly, shallow and swampy, with its beautiful bridge. No more burning, I promise myself, and I swim in the other direction, west, across to the rapids, where it's possible to climb out and lie on the rocks where we often make picnics, taking the food across by canoe: tomatoes, fresh bread, onions, cheese, beer, and fruit. Farther up, we poured in the ashes of my brother and his wife after they died in the crash. But Michael and I are two heads now, moving along like water rats on the surface of this black water, the house back in the trees, where it looks like something we have allowed to happen, containing only tolerance and a hundred after-dinner dances when the table has been pushed aside. Here, while Maryann lives her life in prison, we have been collecting meals, group and solo swims, games of badminton, flowers and vegetables, children and friends, dogs and jokes, hearts and charades, joy and grief.

Chronology

March 13, 1950	William Acker is born, Illinois.
November 4, 1959	Maryann Acker is born, Arizona.
March 1978	William and Maryann meet.
April 29, 1978	William and Maryann marry.
May 28, 1978	A gun is stolen from Maryann's neighbor.
June 1, 1978	William and Maryann fly to Honolulu.
June 10, 1978	Joe Leach is kidnapped and left at Hanauma Bay.
June 20, 1978	Larry Hasker is shot and killed at Hanauma Bay.
	Maryann and William fly to Los Angeles.
June 25, 1978	While hitchhiking, Maryann and William are picked up by Cesario

	Arauza. Arauza's body is found with two gunshot wounds to the head, off Interstate 5 near Los Angeles.
June 25, 26, 28, 1978	Maryann and William commit robberies in California.
June 28, 1978	Maryann Acker is arrested in Long Beach, California.
July 1, 1978	William Acker turns himself in, Yuma, Arizona.
January 29, 1979	Following a jury-waived trial in Los Angeles, Maryann is found guilty of murder in the Arauza case.
	William pleads nolo contendere and is convicted of first-degree murder and robbery in a separate trial.
March 9, 1979	William tells L.A. Detective William Ahn, "There's a body in Hawaii. Maryann did it and she did the one here too."
March 13, 1979	Detective Ahn calls Detective Jimon You in Honolulu.
March–July 1979	William begins testifying as a jailhouse informant for the L.A. County District Attorney's Office.
July 13, 1979	William is sentenced to a life term of imprisonment with the possibility of parole after seven years.
July 18, 1979	Maryann is sentenced to a life term of imprisonment with the possibility of parole after seven years.
1981	Charles Marsland becomes Honolulu's first elected district attorney.

	Hawaii enacts rules of evidence allowing spouses to testify against each other.
August 19, 1981	Maryann is indicted for the murder of Larry Hasker.
March 9, 1982	William signs a plea agreement with DA Marsland. He pleads guilty to the robbery of Larry Hasker. The DA grants him transactional immunity at trial and abandons all other counts against him.
March 31, 1982	Maryann is convicted of kidnapping, robbery in the first degree, unauthorized control of a propelled vehicle, murder, and burglary in the first degree in the Larry Hasker case.
May 24, 1982	William is sentenced to twenty years and placed in witness protection.
	Maryann is sentenced by Judge Au to life with the possibility of parole after a mandatory minimum term of ten years.
December 1982	Hawaii's parole board reestablishes Maryann's term to a mandatory minimum of thirty years.
May 2, 1991	William admits sole responsibility for both the Hasker and Arauza murders.
August 15, 2000	Michael Brennan, Maryann's lawyer, petitions the State of Hawaii to vacate Maryann's 1982 conviction.

October 25–26, 2005	Maryann's hearing at circuit court, Honolulu, takes place.
January 2006	Maryann's 1982 conviction is vacated. The State of Hawaii appeals.
July 2007	Maryann Acker is still in prison at the California Institute for Women in Corona. She is awaiting a decision from the Hawaii Supreme Court on the state's appeal of her vacated conviction. She must also wait for parole from California and for the governor's approval of that parole, if it should happen.

Acknowledgments

My parents taught me to care, to think, and to tell, and I am forever grateful for the example they set. I thank my initial readers: Barbara Gowdy, Constance Rooke, Esta Spalding, Kristin Sanders, and Michael Ondaatje. A reader is the best help a writer can have. Each of these infused the story with insight, ideas, and perspective. I thank Sara Collins, in Honolulu, who kept me in touch with the legal maneuverings there and helped me find people who were lost, along with records and articles in various archives. I thank Michael Brennan and Dan Weiss and the others who have represented Maryann in her legal efforts over many years. I thank them for that and for being helpful to me. I thank Bill and Sakurako Fisher for particular kindness during the writing of this book, and Susie Schlesinger for being there and continuing. I thank Susan Renouf at McClelland & Stewart, and Ann Close at Pantheon, editors with heart. Then I thank Ellen Levine, my more than agent, who cares about content and meaning and getting it right. I thank Michael, again, as my partner in life and the one who encouraged me and listened to me think and helped me seek out the bone truth of my connection to Maryann Acker, who is the most important person of all to thank. Thank you, Maryann.